Fearrington

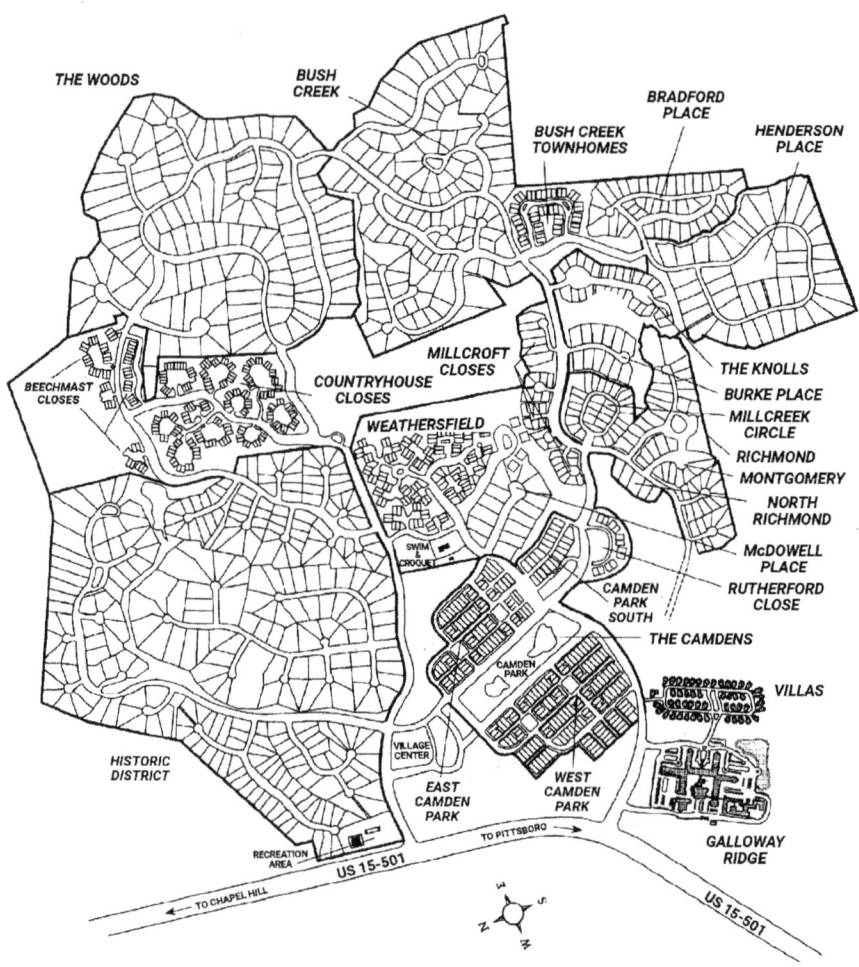

# Fearrington
*Creating an English-Style Village
in the Carolina Countryside*

BILL ARTHUR

McFarland & Company, Inc., Publishers
*Jefferson, North Carolina*

**Frontispiece:** Map of Fearrington Village noting the different neighborhoods (adapted from Fearrington Directory with permission).

ISBN (print) 978-1-4766-9461-0
ISBN (ebook) 978-1-4766-5273-3

LIBRARY OF CONGRESS AND BRITISH LIBRARY
CATALOGUING DATA ARE AVAILABLE

Library of Congress Control Number 2024034422

© 2024 Bill Arthur. All rights reserved

*No part of this book may be reproduced or transmitted in any form or by any means, electronic or mechanical, including photocopying or recording, or by any information storage and retrieval system, without permission in writing from the publisher.*

Front cover image: The main entrance to Fearrington Village with Belted Galloway cattle in the field
(photograph by the author)

Printed in the United States of America

*McFarland & Company, Inc., Publishers
Box 611, Jefferson, North Carolina 28640
www.mcfarlandpub.com*

Dedicated to Kathy Doherty

# Table of Contents

*Acknowledgments* ix
*Preface* 1
*Timeline* 7
*Introduction* 11

One. The Beginning 15
Two. Family and Leadership 27
Three. Partnership 42
Four. Open for Business 55
Five. *The New Yorker* 69
Six. Growth and Change 76
Seven. The Village, the Inn, and More 96
Eight. Gardens and Friendships 126
Nine. Getting Booze to Fearrington: Legislative Legerdemain 136
Ten. Problems, Threats, Tensions, Good Works 141
Eleven. The Future 150

*Appendix: Documents Related to Fearrington Village* 161
*Author's Note on Sources* 173
*Chapter Notes* 177
*Bibliography* 183
*Index* 185

# Acknowledgments

Many people contributed to the completion of this history and the cooperation, the eagerness, of Fearrington residents and others was simply amazing. In effect, I had dozens of researchers for this book.

I fear I will leave someone out, and if so, I apologize profusely. But first of all, thanks to everyone quoted—they are listed in the sources—especially R.B. Fitch, who sat for several interviews, usually at one of his favorite spots, a table at the Roost.

Many thanks to Jess Fearrington, who not only provided facts and memories but also photographs.

Many thanks to Jason Sullivan, Dan Garrett, and Angela Plummer and the rest of the staff at the Chatham County Planning Department who helped me dig through the department files on Fearrington. Also, to Lindsay Ray, clerk to the Chatham County Board of Commissioners, and county attorney Bob Hagemann.

Special thanks to Warren (Gus) Reed, who clued me in to census designated places and how to find them on the Census Bureau website, and to Michael Crowell, who explained to me the intricacies of local bills and North Carolina alcoholic beverage laws. His expertise was especially crucial as no one with the North Carolina Alcoholic Beverage Control Commission ever responded to my repeated calls and emails seeking information. And to Harmony Taylor of Law Firm Carolinas for explaining state law on the relationship of developers and HOAs.

Thanks also go to Pandora Pascal and Chance Mashburn of the county board of elections staff, Bob Steen, who filled me in on the incorporation debate, and Carol Kurtz, who helped me with the Fearrington Homeowners Assocation files and a video.

Also, Natalie Condoret and Brigitte Condoret, Todd Chatterton,

# Acknowledgments

Watson Fitts, Peter Mock, Wendy Moses, Donna Mears, Cassidy Bright, and C.J. Robinson and my buddies in my men's history club, Matt Runcie, Steve Kutay, Vince Tollers, George Lankevich, Doug Rhodes, Bob Pearson, John Vessey, Dave Chapman, and Paul Johnson, who suggested contacts and even dug up the item about longevity in the village. Thanks to Wendy Snodgrass, Steve Stewart, Steve Gambino, Tracy Bailey, Sam Grist, Sally Earnest, Bunny Shillitoe, Kim Parke, and Marcie Ver Ploeg.

Thanks also to Bill Horner and the staff at the *Chatham News + Record* and the staff at the Chatham Community library and Beth Robinson. Thanks also to Denise Todloski, who adapted the map of the village for use in the book.

Naomi Rosestone and Donald Lokuta took some excellent pictures, and Ed Lallo contributed some beautiful photos. I thank them all.

Thanks to my friends in Fearrington and out who, while not quoted, nevertheless contributed with their own discussions of how they got here and why and their experiences in the village. I believe a reporter learns things sort of by osmosis, absorbing information when you don't even realize you are taking it in. These people provided the atmosphere for learning and the encouragement to keep going, especially Terry Parsons and Richard Chase, who are the reason we chose Fearrington, and Bruce and Diane Birch, Vickie and Ed Crocker, Betty Scher, John Webster, Barbara Lankford, Linda and Mark Luftig, Michael and Joanne Cotter, Ken and Christine Kehrer, Mimi and Joe Woehrel, Terry Eason, Jon Whitney, Tony Daniels, Jane Nash, Tony Carroll, Trisha Meketa and Nino Vinkovic, Bob and Maggie Pearson, Brenda and Brian Ginsberg, Lew Powell, Dannye Romine Powell, Sally and Bruce McMillen, and Warren Ort.

Also, many thanks to Colin Doherty for his valuable advice and help with taking and cropping photographs and to Hollis Doherty for her overall support, encouragement, computer expertise and copy editing. It was invaluable.

Thanks also to my sister-in-law, Ruth Reynolds, and brother-in-law, Hank Reynolds, for their counsel and encouragement.

Thanks to my children, Carol Arthur and David Arthur, for their help and encouragement and technical advice and to their spouses,

## *Acknowledgments*

Noemi Arthur and Jon Danforth. Jon's computer expertise smoothed my way through this project. Thanks also to Sebastian Gimenez for his help with the computer.

Finally, and especially, thanks to my late smart, beautiful, and glorious wife, Kathy Doherty, a supremely skilled editor and writer whose insights, suggestions, and encouragement (and knowledge of the quirks of Word) have been crucial to this project. I am a fortunate man to have benefited from her love, liveliness, and companionship. I miss her every day.

# Preface

The development of Fearrington Village could be an ordinary story—conversion of a farm to houses or stores. It happens all the time. The farmers get old, want to retire, the children don't want to farm, the farmers sell to developers who swoop in, build houses in a few years and leave. As one man told the Chatham County, North Carolina, planning board one night, the land was his 401(k).

R.B. and Jenny Fitch did it differently. Instead of clearing land, building houses and departing with their money, the Fitches took their time. Fearrington is still developing after 50 years in business. And the Fitches stayed, living in Fearrington.

R.B. Fitch says that about 60 percent of his sales come from referrals, word of mouth, and that is how my wife, Kathy Doherty, and I came to the village. Our next-door neighbor in Falls Church, Virginia, Terry Parsons, and his partner, Dick Chase, bought a house in Fearrington and encouraged us to check it out. We came, we saw, we were conquered.

When residents were asked in a 2020 community survey what they enjoyed most about the village, almost 75 percent responded that it was the attractiveness of the village. That's what Kathy and I saw. Fearrington is different from the ordinary subdivision. Describing how it is different taxes this writer's vocabulary. Like Fearrington, many other residential developments have nice houses, friendly and helpful neighbors, the amenities common to modern America. But Fearrington somehow puts all these together in a different way—more aesthetically pleasing, with trees and trails and gardens and quiet, houses pleasingly placed adjoining a farm with cows and goats and chickens and, I think, a stronger sense of community than your average subdivision.

# Preface

Ginny Gregory, who was Fearrington's horticulturist for several years, left employment at the village in 1996 after her friend and boss Jenny Fitch died. She had never lived in the village and thought she never would. But she moved to it in 2021.

"It's community," she told me. "I know every single person on the street. I've been here a year and a half. I walk dogs with them. I talk with them. We exchange recipes.... How in the world did I acclimate to this? Because there are trees, because there are pathways, because there's a gathering center" with a nurse on board.

Some people who leave come back. Emily Silverman lived in Fearrington from 2011 until 2018 when she and her husband moved near Wilmington to be close to the beach. But when her husband died, she didn't want to stay there without him, so she moved back to Fearrington, where she still had many friends. "I like the trees and hills, the interesting people, Fearrington Cares, the Duke Center for Living, McIntyre's [bookstore], the many nice places to walk in nature, the weather," she said. "It just feels more like home than where I was."

A bridge in Jenny's Park in snow (photograph by Ed Lallo, Lallo Photography, www.LalloPhotography.com).

*Preface*

I decided someone needed to write a history of the place, especially talking to key figures in its history before it is too late. Already Jenny Fitch, architect Jon Condoret, and project manager Robert Flynn, whom I will discuss later, have died. R.B. Fitch turned 90 in 2023. The wisdom, the energy, the creativity, and, perhaps above all, the patience of these people who thought of community as much as profit created the village. What follows is my attempt to put into words how Fearrington came to be and what makes the place special.

A number of people have written short papers on the history of the village, which were very useful. Many go back to the 1700s, tracing the owners of the land that is now Fearrington through the years—who bought it, who sold it to whom and so on. Nothing wrong with it, but it seemed to me like the "begats" in the King James version of Genesis—something to skip over. I wanted to write about conversion of that farmland into a residential and commercial community, who did it and how, more thoroughly than anyone else had done.

I also saw Fearrington Village as a story on a local level of what was going on in the state and the nation, a place where change happens. People moving into Fearrington from out of state are part of the reason that the South has grown from about 27 percent of the U.S. population in 1960 to almost 35 percent in 2019.

North Carolina has for years been considered one of the more progressive states in the South, though many contend the progress has been, as one writer put it, "timid and modest," and by 2023 had even regressed. But Fearrington for sure helped moderate the conservative politics of Chatham County and the Raleigh–Durham–Chapel Hill region. It helped urbanize, or perhaps suburbanize, Chatham County just as the state and nation were growing more urban. And as the population of urbanizing northeast Chatham County expanded, a stark political contrast grew between the rural and urban areas of the county—again, the same contrast that exists in the state and the nation.

This urbanizing South with rising incomes and greater diversity also fostered the arts in the region so that "the South in cultural terms hardly resembles the region that Mencken famously referred

# Preface

to in 1917 as the 'Sahara of the Bozart,'" writes Peter A. Coclanis, director of the Global Research Institute at the University of North Carolina at Chapel Hill, referring to H.L. Mencken, the American writer and cultural critic of the 20th century.

So I really start in 1974, when Fitch bought the land from Jesse Fearrington. I approached R.B. in 2021, saying I wanted to write a book about this lifelong project of his. He was skeptical, saying he didn't think there was enough material for a book. I said it won't be *War and Peace*, but, like it or not, he has become a key figure in the development of Chatham County and the region, and I'd like to give it a go. He didn't say no. In fact, he sat for several interviews, mostly in his preferred spot, the Roost, the Fearrington Village beer garden. Just as important, he opened the door for me to talk to other key people in the development of Fearrington—his daughters Keebe and Kelley, his son Greg, Laura Morgan, Dan Sears, Theresa Chiettini. He also released to me the series of three interviews he did in 2011 with the Southern Oral History Program at the University of North Carolina at Chapel Hill, which were supposed to be embargoed until his death. Many of his comments from those interviews are published here for the first time.

I had dozens of collaborators on this project, people in Fearrington and out. They encouraged my writing and offered memories and suggestions. You want to know more about the original land sale? Talk to Paul Messick. You want to know about the flowers? You've got to talk to Ginny Gregory. Want to know about liquor-by-the-drink? Talk to Howard Lee.

Any history is an approximation of what actually happened, and there can be many opportunities for misunderstandings or error. For that reason, I submitted drafts of my chapters to R.B. and other key figures for their review, to check the facts. Opinions and analysis are mine or belong to the people quoted, and any errors are mine.

Throughout the book I refer to various Fearrington neighborhoods. While they will be familiar to many Fearrington residents, they may not be familiar to everyone and certainly not to non-residents. For that reason, I have included a map that the reader may wish to consult. Basically, Fitch started building in the north

*Preface*

end of the farm, in what is now called the Historic District, and gradually worked his way roughly clockwise through the property, to the Countryhouse Closes (a close, by the way, is a cul-de-sac), the Woods, Bush Creek, Weathersfield, the Camdens, the Knolls, Montgomery, and Richmond.

As my aim was to appeal to a general reader, I decided not to use footnotes. They can hamper the flow of the text and are the devil to keep track of, which makes me all the more admiring of professional historians and other writers who choose to use them. There is a section on sources at the end of the text which will explain my sourcing in more detail. Suffice to say, my interviews were crucial to this project, and people were happy to speak to me. Why not? They have an interesting story to tell.

# Timeline

Adapted from a timeline produced by Fearrington Homeowners Association and Neville (Tony) Daniels. Used by permission.

Early inhabitants of Chatham County included Iroquoian and Siouan Indians, who were followed by Scottish, English, and German settlers.

- **1771**—Chatham County established and named for William Pitt, the elder, "The Great Commoner," and first Earl of Chatham and prime minister of Great Britain from 1766 to 1768.
- **1787**—Pittsboro established and named for William Pitt the younger, British prime minister 1783–1801, 1804–06.
- **1820**—The Cole farmhouse was built by William Cole, Jr., and a family cemetery still lies by Windstone. (This road was part of the old Chapel Hill Road from Pittsboro during the 1800s.)
- **1875**—E.M. Fearrington married Adelaide Cole, inherited the farm and named it "Eureka Farms."
- **1925**—Fearrington dairy barn for 30 cows approved in May.
- **1927**—Fearrington House built by John "Bun" Fearrington (front porch added about 1939 and in 1947 a two-story addition for Jesse Fearrington, Sr., and Willa).
- **1961**—Fitch Creations, Inc., established in Carrboro as a remodeling and landscaping business.
- **1963**—Fearrington Farm had more than 100 dairy cows, half Guernsey and half Holstein.
- **1973**—Jesse Fearrington, Sr., raises more than 34,000 broiler chickens.
- **1974**—In September, Chatham County Commissioners rezone Fearrington land from residential-agricultural to conditional

## Timeline

use for a planned unit development. In November, R.B. Fitch agrees to purchase land from Fearrington.

**1975**—Fearrington tennis courts built.

**1976**—First Fearrington Village houses open to public on Matchwood. Bill and Moreton Neal open La Residence restaurant in the Fearrington House.

**1977**—R.B. Fitch publishes first of a series of occasional newsletters. Eight issues published through 1979.

**1978**—Playground opens. The Neals move La Residence to Chapel Hill.

**1979**—Jon Condoret is retained for architectural guidance: he designs, and Jenny Fitch decorates, and Fitch Creations builds a solar dream house for *Better Homes and Gardens* magazine. For the next few years the trio creates homes that are featured in such magazines as *Family Circle, Good Housekeeping* and *Southern Living*.

**1980**—Fearrington Homeowners Association becomes a functioning entity. By the end of the year there are 126 houses in Phases I and II and 31 in Phase III. The Fearrington House Restaurant is opened.

**1981**—Architect Jon Condoret goes to work for Fitch full-time. First FHA newsletter published. R.B. Fitch designates the field at Windstone and Turtle Run as a recreation area.

**1982**—Fearrington Wastewater Treatment System comes online. The first four phases of the village, the Historic District, are completed. A basketball court is built at the recreation area. The village center begins redevelopment—the milking barn is converted into shops (now the Dovecote), a corn crib becomes the Roost Beer Garden, the packhouse eventually becomes the Belted Goat, the old hay barn is converted into a meeting and function space. Nearby Jordan Lake becomes fully operational, adding more recreational amenities.

**1983**—Fitch starts running a one-inch ad for Fearrington Village in *The New Yorker*. The Swim & Croquet Club opens. The Market, selling groceries, hardware, newspapers, wine and more, is established in the old granary. It includes a deli and

## *Timeline*

a café serving breakfast, lunch and dinner. Countryhouse Townhomes construction begins. Swim & Croquet Club completed. Fitch buys Belted Galloway cows with white stripes in their middle. They grow in number over the years, becoming iconic figures featured in many ads.

**1984**—Fearrington restaurants permitted to sell beer and wine.

**1986**—The Fearrington House Inn is opened with 14 rooms.

**1987**—Fitch introduces The Woods, a new neighborhood with larger, more upscale homes. These houses are outside the planned unit development (PUD).

**1988**—Weathersfield section approved, to be constructed in the 1990s.

**1989**—R.B. donates the Swim & Croquet Club to its members, who formed it into a separate corporation. The FHA accepts Fitch's offer to build the Gathering Place on two-plus acres. McIntyre's bookstore opens. Fearrington residents rise up to quash a proposed highway bypass that would run through Fearrington.

**1990**—The Gathering Place opens in February. The FHA Planning Committee suggests a study of incorporation. A preliminary study is conducted, but further study is rejected by 88 percent of 450 residents who voted at the annual meeting in November.

**1991**—Camden Park begins with 209 single-family units. Chatham County approves increasing the PUD to 1,602 units with the inclusion of the Bush Creek area of 160 units on R.B. Moore land parcel.

**1993**—The FHA board expands from seven to nine members. Fearrington now totals 744-plus units.

**1995**—Jenny Fitch dies. Fitch Creations moves into present administrative offices. East Camden and Weathersfield townhomes are completed. Fearrington House Restaurant permitted to sell mixed drinks.

**1996**—Back-to-back snow and ice storms hit Fearrington. Hurricane Fran strikes in early September. Project manager Robert Flynn estimates that 100-plus homes were damaged. More than 900 units exist in village at year-end. The Gathering Place is expanded.

# Timeline

**1997**—Camden Park created as a memorial for Jenny Fitch with her favorite plants and trees, now often referred to as Jenny's Park.

**1998**—The FHA office opens. Fitch Creations and the FHA announce that two mail kiosks—Smokehouse and Camden—will be built. The FHA board unanimously endorses a 25-mile-per-hour speed limit throughout the village.

**1999**—Special Olympics bocce matches take place at Fearrington with participants from all over the world. "Farmer Bob" Strowd hired as full-time farm manager.

**2000**—A surprise snowstorm blankets Fearrington with more than 20 inches of snow. Two other storms follow within a week. Fearrington Cares created from the merger of Home Care Connection and Stay Put for Now.

**2001**—Widening of U.S. 15–501 begins. FHA board unanimously opposes the nearby Briar Chapel subdivision, the first time it has taken a position on an issue. The board votes to spend $11,000 to upgrade the playground and make it safer.

**2002**—FHA website opens. Tolls are eliminated on phone calls between Pittsboro, Chapel Hill, and Durham. R.B. Fitch withdraws permission to hunt deer on his land, ending consideration of herd management.

**2003**—Fitch buys several Tennessee fainting goats. Ground is broken for Galloway Ridge.

**2004**—A deer census determines there are 131 deer in Fearrington, but the FHA board says it cannot cull the herd because of high costs and land limitations. R.B. Fitch offers to build and donate a new office for Fearrington Cares behind the Gathering Place.

**2005**—Residents again reject further consideration of incorporation 52 to 48 percent. New Fearrington Cares office opens. Galloway Ridge and the Duke Center for Living open. Widening of 15–501 completed.

**2011**—Henderson Place is added to the village, though is not part of the PUD.

**2022**—Fitch announces plans for Granville, a new neighborhood of 52 acres off of Millcroft at the southern end of the village.

# Introduction

Driving south on U.S. 15–501 from Chapel Hill, on the east side of the road about seven miles out, you might easily dismiss the sign for Fearrington Village as a hyped-up name for a farm, not the location of a major residential subdivision. You'll see open fields behind a white fence corralling a few black and white cows, goats, and perhaps a donkey. You'll see a silo, a barn, and a chicken coop, and the only house easily visible will be the old white, colonial revival farmhouse of the dairy farm the place once was.

But if you turn left onto Village Way, you'll begin to see houses of earth-toned wood with skylights and clerestory windows and straight lines and decks, neatly spaced, tucked in among trees, many trees. If you then take the first right on a road lined with tall Zelkova trees, you'll enter the village with its bookstore, boutique, spa, and combination restaurant, coffee shop, and wine store. You'll also see a luxury inn and a five-star restaurant. (Fearrington Village isn't a gated community, so you are free to roam.)

You'll be entering a vibrant community of some 1,500 homes and 2,700 residents with its fields and parkland, walking paths, gardens, swimming pool, tennis courts (with pickleball lines), bocce ball court, croquet court. Fearrington Village is a major residential community, which, while not age-restricted, has drawn retirees from all over the country and the world, attracted to the region because of high quality health care at the University of North Carolina in nearby Chapel Hill and Duke University in Durham, Raleigh-Durham International Airport, quality entertainment and sports venues, good restaurants, good climate—or maybe they just want to be near children or grandchildren who live and work in the area.

It's also a safe community. The Chatham County sheriff's office

# Fearrington

**Zelkova trees on the entry road to the village center (photograph by Ed Lallo, Lallo Photography, www.LalloPhotography.com).**

received only 154 crime reports from Fearrington between 2015 and mid–2023, and more than half of those involved fraud, such as credit card fraud or other scams. "Knowing the stats for other subdivisions of similar size, I'd assess that Fearrington Village is a safe community," Randall Rigsbee, spokesman for the Chatham County sheriff's office, wrote in an email.

But Fearrington Village isn't only a residential community. It also is a vacation spot with a world-class inn and an events center with weddings, corporate events, and parties almost every weekend in the revamped old barn or elsewhere on the grounds.

"Nothing about this place is ordinary," a reporter for the *News & Observer* of Raleigh once wrote. "Fearrington is one of those magical places where you easily lose your worries and your bearings."

He was staying at the luxurious Fearrington Inn, where one can easily be transported out of ordinary life.

But even for Fearrington residents there are many diversions from the routine. There is a bridge club, mahjong club, investment club, poker club, garden club, genealogy group and, of course, Democrat and Republican clubs. There's even a yacht club—no boat required—and assorted wine clubs, book clubs, movie groups and

*Introduction*

**Fearrington House Restaurant and Inn decorated for Christmas (photograph by Colin Doherty).**

more. There is a concert series. Fearrington Village is a walkable community with more than four miles of trails and gravel paths winding through the forests and neighborhoods, which encourages comradeship: one may just wave a casual hello at a passing stroller or stop and talk for a while with friend or stranger. And there's a farmers' market every Tuesday throughout the year.

The village has a certain esprit de corps. Retirees who previously may have sacrificed quality of life to live near their jobs were now free to choose Fearrington because that's just where they wanted to live in their personal pursuit of happiness.

For some people, Fearrington is a second home. But it also is the primary home for many retirees, so the village doesn't empty out every morning with people going to work. People can stay home and follow their interests.

Fearrington Village also has a non-profit organization, Fearrington Cares, that provides volunteer educational services, transportation, minor health care for residents and live-at-home assistance.

All this has developed from the dairy farm Fearrington once was, guided by the vision of developer R.B. Fitch, an open-minded and forward-looking man whose business acumen was supplemented

# Fearrington

**The farmers' market, every Tuesday at Fearrington Village (photograph by Bill Arthur).**

by his wife, Jenny, whose attention to the flowers and food and the finer things helped make Fearrington the comfortable place it is today. The Fitches are so revered in the community that the Fearrington Homeowners Association presented them a "Visionary Award" in 2021 for creating "a truly unique residential community that is embraced by all."

But it wasn't easy getting Fearrington Village to where it is today.

# One

# The Beginning

Fearrington Village has been around for almost 50 years at this writing. It is entrenched in northeast Chatham County, a residential community with a farm backdrop that looks as natural as the fields and trees and gardens that inhabit it. It looks inevitable.

It wasn't.

Its origin lies in the decisions of Jesse Fearrington and his son, Jesse Jr. The land had been in the Fearrington family since 1859, when Adelaide Cole and her husband, Edward M. Fearrington, Jesse Fearrington's grandfather, inherited it from Adelaide's father, Elijah Cole. While we spell the name Fearrington today, the family a century or two back had some alternatives, such as Farrington or Ferrington. John Andrew Fearrington, the first Fearrington in North Carolina, held land grants under both spellings, so perhaps he decided to combine them and come up with Fearrington, speculated Jesse Fearrington, Jr. Research back to England suggests the name was once even spelled Ffarrington, he said.

"Maybe they were just illiterate on how to spell their name, who knows?" he said.

The Cole family had owned the land since 1786 when William Cole, Sr., bought it from John Oldham for $80. The Coles farmed tobacco, cotton and corn. John Bunyan Fearrington, Jesse's father, had converted the farm, called Eureka Farms, to dairy in the 1930s, and the other fields gradually returned to their natural forested state. Jesse was the sixth generation of his family to run the farm.

Dairy farming is hard work. You get up at 3 a.m. and round up the cows, then milk them. You're done about 6:30 when you get breakfast, and then you do the same thing all over again at 2:30 p.m., every day, rain or shine, seven days a week, 365 days a year. Milk cows

# Fearrington

don't take holidays. And the cows must be fed, their stalls cleaned, the milk carefully handled. In 1974 Jesse Sr. had been running the farm for years, and now he was 54 and thinking of the future. He went to Atlanta for a serious talk with his son, who was working for Bell South and had concluded as a teenager that dairy farming was not for him. He went to North Carolina State University and got a degree in computer science.

"He came down and he said, 'It's just me on the farm now, and it's hard to find labor,'" said Jesse Jr., better known as Jess. "'I have been talking with R.B. Fitch, and R.B. wants to buy the property and create a development.' He asked me how I felt about that. I said, 'Dad, I think that's just wonderful.'" Nor did Jess's sister want to take over the 650-acre farm with its forests, cropland and pastures. Jesse Sr. took steps to unload the farm, selling his 105 dairy cows, which produced an average of almost 700 gallons of milk each day. He also phased out of his broiler chicken business.

The land didn't go right away to R.B. Fitch. Jesse Fearrington initially sold an option to the Bell Design Group of Raleigh, a partnership of Richard Bell and Louis Smith, who sought a builder capable of handling the many slopes and valleys on the property and who also accepted their concept for the land: mostly single-family housing, but also single-family attached housing plus a village with a school, a church, a crafts area and possibly a convenience

Jesse Fearrington, Sr. (Jesse Fearrington, Jr., Collection).

*One. The Beginning*

The dairy barn at Fearrington, 1953 (Jesse Fearrington, Jr., Collection).

store, but importantly, also retaining aspects of the farm. Here was the seed of what would become the Fearrington planned unit development.

They found their man in Fitch, who had built homes in previous locations in Chatham County, namely the Chatham development on Mann's Chapel Road and Polk's Landing. At first, he was reluctant.

"I was approached by a real estate person who wanted to know if I was interested in the Fearrington farm, and I said no, it's just too much," Fitch said. "They went away and were unable to find a buyer, so they came back and talked again." After a time in England as a U.S. Air Force officer, he had retained a vision of a walkable English country village with houses surrounding open space, parks, recreational areas, and stores, a vision shared by his wife, Jenny. "We agreed to buy it over time," contingent on getting it rezoned for a mixed-use development, both residential and commercial.

He did some due diligence, paying graduate students at UNC $2,000 to study whether his concept was viable. "They said it wouldn't be very smart," he said. Fitch put the study away in a desk drawer. "This isn't something the bankers need to see," he thought. "I just felt like it would work out."

# Fearrington

Bell Design's option expired in October 1974, and in November Fitch agreed to pay $1 million for the land, buying it in sections of about 40 acres every year or two, paying Jesse Fearrington $40,000 a year plus interest. It was largely borrowed money. "I probably had $2,000 in it of real money," he said. One of his lenders was NCNB, which vouched for Fitch's creditworthiness in a 1978 letter to county officials, saying, "Mr. Fitch has been a most valuable customer of North Carolina National Bank for many years. During the years Mr. Fitch has banked with us, we have had numerous occasions to lend him money for various purposes, including six loans for land development purposes. These loans and all other banking relationships with us have always been handled as agreed."

"I used to drive by Fearrington Farm when I was a boy," Fitch told the *Chapel Hill News* years later. "We'd go to the beach in South Carolina for vacation, and this was the prettiest place on the whole trip. It never dawned on me that someday I'd have the privilege of owning it."

Aerial view of the Fearrington Farm, circa 1945 (Jesse Fearrington, Jr., Collection).

## One. The Beginning

Marrying a village with shops and residences was radical for Chatham County at the time and required a new way of thinking. So Fitch proposed a planned unit development, or PUD, the first of its kind in Chatham County, and one of the first in the state.

A planned unit development is designed to provide a mix of land uses—single-family homes and townhouses combined with commercial development, open spaces, and recreational facilities. In return for the open spaces and other amenities, the developer can build houses at greater density than in a standard subdivision. While that may be of benefit to the developer, it can also benefit the community. "The typical single-family subdivision costs the town more in services than it returns in tax revenue, while the well-conceived PUD could return more to the town in revenue than it costs in services," wrote Maxwell Huntoon, author of a book on PUDs for the Urban Land Institute.

"I wanted to do something that will last a long time," Fitch said.

"It was the first large subdivision that the county had ever seen," said Paul Messick, whose law firm handled details of the eventual sale.

"The project was way ahead of its time with the notion of mixing low density residential with some variety in housing type, with a unique village and agriculture bent," said Mark Ashness, principal with CE Group, a planning, engineering, and survey firm with offices in Raleigh and Chatham Park. "In some ways I believe Fearrington was the innovator for this style of mixed-use, at least in the South."

Geographically smack dab in the middle of the state, Chatham County was quiet, off the beaten path. It lost out for the location of the state capital by one vote. It also might have been the site for the University of North Carolina, but school officials decided Pittsboro had too many saloons, which would have a bad influence on the students, according to a 1970 Chatham County land development study. In addition, "citizens residing in the neighborhood of Chapel Hill offered what appeared to be the greater inducements [money] than those made by the people of Chatham, and the university was located in the neighboring county of Orange." Chatham County was also to have been the site for one of the first railroads in the state, but

**Fearrington**

local farmers feared trains would kill their cattle and petitioned legislators to keep the "iron horse" away. Today, "it seems that in the raucous economic growth, the echoes of the past are mostly faint" in Chatham, to quote local historian Warren Reed. There are "no ante-bellum plantations to visit, no battlefields to tour."

Chatham County was largely rural in 1974, population about 30,600, concentrated in the small towns of Pittsboro, population 1,447, Siler City, 4,689, and Goldston, 364. Unlike today, there was no Briar Chapel subdivision, no Governors Club, no Powell Place, not much of anything between Chapel Hill and Pittsboro, and the main highway, 15–501, was a two-lane road with no turn-lane into Fearrington. Phone numbers were divided—either Pittsboro or Chapel Hill—and a call to a neighbor across the street could be long-distance. There were no stoplights between Chapel Hill and Fearrington, and not even one at 15–501 and Village Way, the main entrance to the village, until residents petitioned for one. The closest grocery store was in Carrboro, and there were no eating places between Fearrington and Chapel Hill or Pittsboro.

"It was quite a ways to come down here, especially on a two-lane road," said Fearrington resident Doug Zabor, who handled some of the initial publicity for the village. "The distance from Chapel Hill was a real negative."

Chatham County was also poor, ranking in the bottom quartile for median family income in the state. That suggested home buyers would have to come from wealthier Orange, Durham, and Wake counties. Still, R.B. Fitch was excited. He had a plan, but could he execute it? Opposition was strong and would continue for years. And he needed to get the PUD approved by county officials, many of whose constituents saw the proposal as the ruination of the county.

"It was going to be the worst thing that ever happened to Chatham County," said former county planning director Keith Megginson, paraphrasing critics of the plan. "There wasn't water. It was taking farmland and turning it into this development. And the road was two lanes, and traffic was going to be bad. Just everything you can imagine was going to be terrible."

## One. The Beginning

In a county where, to this day, some people feel crowded if they can see a neighbor's house from their own, the development would be too dense, opponents said. County regulations "should not be changed for anyone to allow any further density of the growth of Chatham County," said a petition to county commissioners signed by 464 people.

"There has always been a segment of U.S. opinion that views dense urban living as inherently dystopian," *New York Times* columnist Paul Krugman has said. Blame Thomas Jefferson, one of the greatest influencers, to use a modern term, in American history, who extolled the rural life.

"Cultivators of the earth are the most valuable citizens," he wrote. "They are the most vigorous, the most independent, the most virtuous." Cities were a sore on the body politic. "I view great cities as pestilential to the morals, the health and the liberties of man," he wrote. The view of the country as virtuous and the city as sinful is a persistent trope that, whether recognized or not, played in the background of the Fearrington debate, and it persists in American culture.

Some local farmers, land rich but cash poor, envisioned selling their own land some day and so backed Fearrington's planned sale. But opposition was vehement. Jesse Fearrington received hate mail, some from people he thought were friends, saying "vile, nasty things" about him and complaining that his sale would lead to slums, "a ghetto" in Chatham County, recalled Jesse Jr.

The editor of the *Pittsboro Herald* was a particular thorn in Fitch's side, leading "a real fight to keep me out of doing any development at Fearrington," Fitch recalled.

The PUD called for some 1,800 to 2,000 houses (eventually 1,602 homes), some of which would be closer together than under standard zoning. In return the developer would have to provide open spaces and amenities. Opponents questioned how it would fit into the county's plans for growth. What about water and sewer service? What about the impact on traffic? Did Chatham County have a sophisticated enough planning department to oversee the developer? Will it return in taxes what it will cost the county for the impact on roads and schools and police and fire protection? Was there even a market for such a development?

While Richard Bell had a good reputation as a landscape architect, he wasn't a proven developer. The project needed a developer who could handle the hills and ravines on the land, and R.B. Fitch was relatively unknown. Even though he had been building houses in the county since the early 1960s the *Pittsboro Herald* said it was unable in the time available "to obtain any information about Fitch."

"Clearly, the Fearrington PUD is the most controversial and the most complex residential development to date in Chatham County," then–county planning director Michael Surface wrote in 1978.

Of course, cities are the original mixed-use development, and people have been living above the store for centuries. Large U.S. cities began some restrictions on land use in the late 19th century. In 1885, San Francisco banned public laundries in certain areas, really a racist tactic to zone out Chinese businesses. The U.S. Supreme Court struck down the law in 1886 as a violation of the 14th Amendment's equal protection clause.

The Industrial Revolution spurred efforts to separate commercial, industrial, and residential operations. The idea was to enable people to live away from the noise, smoke, and smells of the factory. Los Angeles adopted a law in 1909 to restrict areas for heavy industry and commercial operations, and New York City adopted a code in 1916 regulating building heights to limit construction that blocked sunlight and air.

A 1926 U.S. Supreme Court ruling established zoning as a legal and legitimate tool of local government. The Ambler Realty Company of Euclid, Ohio, wanted to lease some of its land to industrial customers, but the village zoned the land for residential use. Ambler sued, claiming its property had been seized without due process, a violation of the U.S. Constitution. The Supreme Court ruled 6–3 that the village zoning ordinance was "a valid exercise of authority," establishing a precedent that spurred zoning throughout the country.

Zoning might have been considered arbitrary or unreasonable 50 or 100 years ago, the court said, but as the advent of automobiles and rapid transit had produced the need for traffic rules, so the nation's increasing urbanization required rules for land use. "While the meaning of constitutional guaranties never varies," the court said, "the scope of their application must expand or contract to meet the new and different conditions which are constantly coming within the field of their operation. In a changing world it is impossible that it should be otherwise."

Today, Houston, Texas, is the largest unzoned city in the country.

The automobile further stoked zoning as it became possible for people to live farther away from work. Thus, the suburbs. What ensued was called Euclidian zoning, allowing one kind of use in each zone—residential or commercial or industrial, for example. It became the standard type of zoning throughout the country, but it often led to urban sprawl and economic and racial segregation.

Some planners began questioning the process. One such person was Robert E. Simon, Jr., the founder of Reston, Virginia, a mixed-use community established in 1964.

"Our present zoning ordinances are largely responsible for the diffusion of our communities into separate, unrelated hunks without focus, identity, or community life," Simon said. "They have helped produce chaos on our highways, monotony in our subdivisions, and ugliness in our shopping centers. They are to blame for the whole neon-lighted wasteland that exists because of the subdivision's separation from commercial and recreational facilities."

While always around, the concept of mixed-use began to burgeon in the 1970s.

"It's probably the hottest thing in planning," said David Godschalk, a professor of city and regional planning at UNC Chapel Hill in an interview with the *News & Observer* of Raleigh in 1992. "It's an attempt to get back into some values we had in small towns before the automobile took over."

Mixed-use reduces traffic and pollution as people need to drive less to work or shop. It can also reduce costs such as fire and police protection and trash collection for towns and counties. Also, Smart Growth America, a non-profit that helps state and local governments deal with growth, estimates that compact mixed-use communities save on infrastructure costs such as roads and sewers compared with large-lot subdivisions. While they enable developers to increase profits, they also can boost tax revenue for local governments.

And they are attractive to homebuyers. "According to estimates, some 33 percent of the population desires to live in a walkable, mixed-use neighborhood, and that's because ... it really offers that sense of community to everyone who's there," said Marie-Claire Burick, president of the Rosslyn Business Improvement District in Arlington, Virginia. The Fearrington plan offered people "country living" while still being close to their jobs in Chapel Hill, Durham or Raleigh, a Chatham County planning document said.

Places like Reston and Fearrington "demonstrate that higher density and controlled mixed-use development is not harmful to homeowners' interests," said William Fischel, professor emeritus of economics and legal studies at Dartmouth College. "Homebuyers in planned communities usually have the security that the community they are buying into will not change without their permission and that of their neighbors."

Still, the concept was new to many in North Carolina, and Fitch and the Bell Design Group helped the county write the PUD regulations, "fashioned after some larger areas that had planned unit developments," Fitch said. County planners and commissioners proceeded cautiously. "There are all sorts of problems inherent in a project of this sort," warned Robert DeMaine, senior regional planner for the area's Triangle J Council of Governments.

The county planning board first considered the plan, technically a request to rezone the land from residential-agricultural to conditional use for a planned unit development in a meeting at the Pittsboro courthouse on July 9, 1974. Jack Leister of the Bell Design Group "showed maps of the existing topography, soils, and vegetation of the area involved," according to the meeting minutes. He estimated that the site would contain 1,800 to 2,000 housing units, or about three units per acre. After some discussion, not specified in the minutes, the board went into a closed session, which would not be legal today and was probably improper even then, to make its decision. They

## One. The Beginning

then recommended approval of the measure 4–0. Jesse Fearrington, the fifth planning board member present, abstained.

The five county commissioners met jointly with the planning board at a public hearing on July 29, 1974. As the item came up for discussion, Jesse Fearrington left his seat with the planning board and sat with the audience. Richard Bell of the Bell Design Group described the farm as "beautiful property with unique characteristics that should be preserved historically." His plan proposed saving all the present facilities of the farm and most of the trees. Audience members questioned the availability of water for the development, the quality of the houses and who would buy them and they sought assurance that the development wouldn't be a burden on the county budget. The commissioners took no action on the measure that night.

The matter came up again at an August 5 commissioners meeting. The Bell Design Group offered more details about the plan, and Jesse Fearrington assured commissioners that he didn't plan any rental units on the property. The development "would be something the county could be proud of," he said.

The county commissioners considered the plan again on August 19, 1974, expressing skepticism.

"I'm concerned about what this development will look like in 10–12 years," chairman June Wrenn said. "This is so much bigger than anything else, there's a lot I don't understand."

Commissioners peppered Fitch with questions about the size of the houses—about 1,300 square feet per house, he said, the water supply—from a utility built by a private firm—and police protection—from the sheriff's department, which would not require a large outlay for more deputies as development will occur over 15 to 20 years, Fitch said. He tried to reassure their concerns about density. "The farm is so beautiful we want to save its look," he said. The board clerk submitted for the record letters from people opposed to the plan.

Commissioners took no action but agreed with Wrenn, who concluded, "I sure learned more tonight than at the public hearing," according to the *Pittsboro Herald*. Continuing their inquiries, the commissioners two days later visited Kildaire Farms in Cary, the state's first PUD.

**Fearrington**

The commissioners took up the matter again on September 16. Some 30 residents of northeast Chatham requested a study to determine the effects of the PUD on the county. Only one person spoke in favor of the PUD, but the commissioners had made up their minds. After some discussion, Commissioner Ben Wimberly moved approval of a resolution declaring Fearrington Farm was "a beautiful property with unique characteristics in historical qualities deserving of preservation." The resolution said the development "would be built around the saving of all the present facilities and most of the trees" and was a good site for residential housing, "but its slopes require a builder who is able to cope with them."

The plan proposed mostly single-family detached housing but also some single-family attached housing "along with a school site, church site, crafts area and perhaps a convenience store. There will be no motel or shopping center." The resolution said the land is "well suited for the establishment of a planned unit development because of its size, topography, road network and geographical location." The motion passed 3–0. Commissioner Earl Thompson abstained, according to the meeting minutes, perhaps because he was a friend of Jesse Fearrington and because he did some construction work for Fitch. Board chairman Wrenn was absent.

An angry citizen, Hubert Oakley, resigned from the county Board of Adjustment in protest. "This decision violates the whole purpose of our zoning code. I think the whole county planning board should resign, too. They've failed in their jobs on this," he said.

But for R.B. Fitch and the Bell Design Group, failure wasn't in the plan.

# Two

# Family and Leadership

Roy Bernice Fitch, Jr., is a patient man. He has been working on a dream for 50 years, and he hasn't finished it. Maybe that's the point. Don't finish it. As he once said, if you're having fun "better just keep on doing it."

The dream is Fearrington Village, the community he and his team at Fitch Creations have created and are still building.

"He calculated at the beginning how many homes he'd need to build to stay busy all his life," said Theresa Chiettini, general manager of the village at Fitch Creations, and set his construction pace accordingly.

He was no newcomer to homebuilding when he started the village in 1974. Born on August 19, 1933, to R.B. Fitch and Katherine McIntyre (which is why the Fearrington bookstore is called McIntyre's), Fitch grew up in a house on tony Franklin Street in Chapel Hill next to the UNC chancellor's house. He's been called R.B. all his life. His father ran the Fitch Lumber Company in Carrboro and was a director of the Bank of Chapel Hill, a position R.B. would later assume before the bank was absorbed by North Carolina National Bank, now Bank of America. As a kid R.B. worked at the lumber company. "I'd go out late afternoon after school, on the weekends, every summer I worked there, 10 cents an hour, and at that time I was overpaid," he joked. He worked there as he got older too. "I was just sort of a gofer," he said.

R.B. went to high school in Chapel Hill and noted that many of his classmates were the children of university professors. "They were smart, they were well traveled, they were exposed in their homes to a lot of intelligent things, so I was up against it trying to keep up with that class." Still, he was president of the student body his senior year.

## Fearrington

He also joined the basketball team. "I was the thirteenth man on a thirteen-person team, and I caught a lot of splinters," he said.

He went to college at UNC, where he graduated in 1955 with a degree in business administration.

"I guess I was a little better than average student, not a hell of a lot better," he said, though he allowed that "math was one of my strong suits. I was in the top 10 percent or 5 percent or something of the class and didn't have any problem getting in Carolina." Majoring in business was "probably not the most well-rounded education a person can get," he said. "I didn't walk away with a well-full of knowledge." But he knew he wanted to be a businessman. "I loved retail; I loved merchandising. I loved the way things fit in a shelf. I loved to see why people buy things, why they don't buy things. I loved helping people."

The Korean War was underway while Fitch was an undergraduate and, like other young American men, he was subject to the draft. He joined the Air Force Reserve Officer Training Corps "so that at least I would be an officer when I went in the service."

After graduation he took pilot training to fly the F-100 Super

**U.S. Air Force F-100 decorated for the Thunderbirds flying team (National Museum of the U.S. Air Force).**

## Two. Family and Leadership

Sabre, the first U.S. fighter jet to achieve sustained supersonic speed. Called "the Hun," for one hundred, the F-100 was "the hottest plane the Air Force had right then," Fitch said. The Air Force's Thunderbirds aerial display team flew it for years. It was a dangerous job. More than a third of the 2,294 F-100s produced were involved in accidents, with 324 pilot deaths.

He took flight training in Florida and then at Webb Air Force Base in Big Spring, Texas, near, well, nothing. (Abilene, the nearest town of any note, is 100 miles east, and there was no interstate in those days.) "I have not found a reason to go back there," he said. "I mean, in the wintertime, in my little old lightweight flight jacket, out preflighting a plane a 6:00 in the morning, cold, tumbleweeds coming across the runway. I thought I was going to freeze to death."

The Air Force told Fitch that because they had trained him to fly the F-100, he had to sign up for a five-year obligation, extending his three-year ROTC requirement. He had already spent 18 months in training and told them, "You've got me 18 more months. I'm not going to sign anything." The Air Force threatened to send him to Goose Bay, Labrador, for his intransigence but instead posted him to the 55th Fighter Bomber squadron at a Royal Air Force base in Wethersfield, England, outside London. Fitch would later name a street in Fearrington for that RAF base, but he added an "a" to make it Weathersfield, lest anyone conclude "R.B. can't spell." (Note: A wether is a castrated male sheep or goat, so Wethersfield could refer to a sheep or goat farm, appropriate for Fearrington Village today.)

In England he shared a house with three other bachelor officers. The flying time was practice, practice, practice, preparation for combat if matters ever came to that. Sometimes they would fly to Libya for training because the weather in England was "socked in all the time," Fitch said. In combat, every plane would have an atomic weapon and a target, he said. "You'd go in about fifty or 100 feet above the ground, then you'd flip up and you'd toss the bomb," he said, lobbing it to make a quick getaway before it exploded.

"It was a marvelous, marvelous time. I would never have gone to England. I would have never had the experience of travel. I'd never been further than Myrtle Beach," he said. "I think everybody ought

**R.B. Fitch in his flight suit, circa 1957 (courtesy R.B. Fitch).**

to be in the service. I think everybody ought to do some sort of community service."

The good times, the coziness and comfort of English villages, never left his mind. "Visually, I just liked England," he said.

Fitch completed his Air Force duty in 1958 and has never piloted a plane since. To continue being a pilot, he said, "you need two things, time and money. I didn't have either."

Returning home, he was thinking of finding a nice girl and getting married. He visited his old fraternity house, found some friends, told them he was looking around. Someone suggested he look up Decia Jeannette Elder, better known as Jenny, a popular girl on campus.

## Two. Family and Leadership

Daughter Keebe Fitch said, "The story that we've been told is he got back from the Air Force, and he went to a party, his fraternity, and said to one of his fraternity brothers, 'I just want to meet a nice person to marry,' and the guy turned around, introduced him to Mom."

The daughter of a Ford dealer in Siler City, Jenny was a campus leader, a cheerleader, president of her Chi Omega sorority, a member of the student government, on the Panhellenic Council, and on the Orientation Committee. She was a graduation marshal and was Miss October in the annual *Yackety Yack* yearbook collection of attractive women. "She was really a cute gal," R.B. said, "vivacious personality, good-looking, had everything."

Even though R.B. was president of his Alpha Tau Omega fraternity his senior year, had served in the student legislature and the Interfraternity Council and had been an orientation counselor, he considered himself "a very secluded guy" compared with Jenny Elder. "My chances here are slim," he thought, but he took his shot and started courting her in her senior year. They had in common that they both were from small North Carolina towns. Siler City was

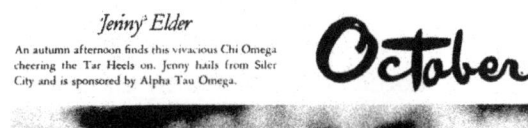

Jenny Elder in the UNC yearbook, *The Yackety Yack*, in 1960.

so small that Jenny's telephone number at home was 79. The switchboard was upstairs in a store downtown, and he remembers calling one time to have the operator tell him Jenny wasn't home because she just saw her walk by the store. After Jenny graduated in 1960 she headed off to Atlanta and worked in Rich's Department store. Fitch felt he wasn't getting anywhere. "I decided, well, I was going to give this thing one more shot. Easter came around, and I sent an orchid, and I said, 'Just thinking about you for Easter, and I want you to have a good Easter.'"

She responded positively. "Well, why don't you come down and see me sometime?" she said. They married that Christmas, 1962, forming a partnership that lasted 33 years and produced three children and Fearrington Village. "I married above myself," R.B. said. And "I believe in flowers."

"He adored her," said Ginny Gregory, a former Fearrington horticulturist and friend.

Unfortunately, Jenny Fitch died of cancer in 1995, but she is revered in the village and left a legacy of fine dining and gardens and hospitality that mark Fearrington today.

In 1961 R.B. Fitch established Fitch Creations, Inc., to do kitchen and bath remodeling and landscaping. Note the choice of a name. Not Fitch Construction or Fitch Remodeling, but Fitch Creations.

He moved into house construction in the mid–1960s, building houses at the Chatham development on Mann's Chapel Road and then in 1971–72 at Polk's Landing on the west side of route 15–501 two and a half miles north of Fearrington Village. He was "trying to build little houses that had character." It was a simpler time, he said. He could get a loan approved in a day and complete a house in six to eight weeks.

Fitch Creations today has some 100–140 employees from real estate agents handling home sales to gardeners to architects to the cooks and sommelier at the Fearrington House Restaurant. It is very much a family enterprise. R.B. remained president as of 2024, with his son, Greg, as vice president, though Greg had begun assuming more duties. Daughter Katherine, better known as Keebe, is secretary and runs the bookstore, and daughter Kelley is assistant treasurer

## Two. Family and Leadership

and marketing director. The company lists 50 shares of Class A voting stock and 950 shares of Class B non-voting stock, and all shares are held in the family.

Real estate developers, like politicians and used car salesmen, are stereotypical sketchy characters in American culture. They are often seen as "big, ugly builders with black hats, mustaches, gold chains and big Cadillacs," the late Robert Toll, co-founder of the Toll Brothers home building company, once said. R.B. Fitch, while not immune from criticism, is the antithesis of that image, not boastful or flashy. He seems almost embarrassed by his prominence in the community and the Raleigh–Durham–Chapel Hill Triangle region.

"He's really a good soul. He's the best part of a southern gentleman," said former Fearrington resident Jill Wargin.

At age 90 (in 2023), Fitch was a hefty six foot one. He walks and works out daily and enjoys crossword puzzles, but he doesn't tackle the *New York Times* Sunday puzzle and the other tougher ones that appear later in the week. "I'm a Monday, Tuesday, Wednesday fellow," he said. "I can only be challenged so much."

He used to enjoy an occasional glass of scotch or wine but said he's pretty much cut back on that, though "I'm not a teetotaler, but close."

He also used to smoke but quit in his 30s. The surgeon general's report on the dangers of smoking had been issued, and he and some friends decided to quit. "If you can go two weeks without smoking you can

R.B. Fitch, June 2023 (photograph by Bill Arthur).

quit," he said. "You've got to get through the two weeks. I'm convinced I wouldn't be here today if I had kept smoking."

He enjoys *Seinfeld* reruns and especially British mysteries on Acorn and Britbox, but not too graphic. "Just the feet [of a corpse] showing through a door," that's enough to get the message, he said.

He used to play golf but stopped in part because one of his best golfing buddies died. They played about once a week. Fitch said he was a bogey player, meaning he could shoot a bit above par, and he enjoyed it. "It's one of the few things you can go and do and be completely removed from everything."

"He doesn't really talk much, and he doesn't really get socially involved," said good friend Luther Hodges, Jr. "He doesn't really want to get out in a crowd. He's quite comfortable with himself, and he stays there."

"I'm not a glad-hander and sort of loquacious fellow," Fitch said. "I'm more of an observer than I am in the middle of things."

While Fitch may be no social butterfly, he has staged events to draw village residents and others to Fearrington. He for years held an annual Christmas party until Robert Flynn, the catalyst for the festivities, died. He's held Easter egg hunts and used to have an annual Halloween party in which staffers carved intricate and artistic pumpkins that people drove from miles around to see. He stopped that party when Covid hit and resumed it on a smaller scale after traffic got jammed in the village, and he worried about people spraining an ankle walking through the village on a dark October night.

He does try to keep the business and social affairs apart and rarely dines with residents. He may have been invited to a resident's home a time or two, he said, "but I'm not sure I went." He would rarely join local golfers on the course.

But he is an amiable fellow, ready with a laugh. "He's just a fun, lively, honest person with a great sense of humor," said long-time friend Gerald Bell. With R.B. "you don't get a fake person, you get an authentic person."

While Fitch says he can't remember details of events of some 40 or 50 years ago, that's typical for anyone. He remains, alert, sharp, in touch as a man many years his junior. While Greg Fitch has taken over more of the daily operations, it's clear where the buck stops. "He's a product of his generation," Greg said. "He's used to being in charge of a company, used to directing people."

"I've always liked to be in charge, being decision-maker," R.B. said. "I dislike committees. I dislike a lot of just *stuff* that gets in the way of making a decision."

He often could be found roaming the grounds, greeting residents and visitors, meeting with staff at the Roost, the village beer garden.

"Before Covid he would come out and shake everybody's hand when they would come," recalled Chris Culbreth, a real estate agent with numerous sales in the village. "He would meet them individually. You know, at his age now he has to be careful, but he has always wanted to know the residents and say hello to them." And people are interested in his doings. There have been rumors that he would remarry, or that he had become a monk and was moving to Asia.

"It's amazing the stories that people come up with," Fitch said.

As for marriage, "I've never thought about getting married again," he said. He has dated and has a lady friend, Catherine, in Winston-Salem. "We just enjoy each other's company," he said.

As a getaway, Fitch has a home "in the middle of nowhere," 90 acres on a mountaintop in Floyd County, Virginia, southwest of Roanoke. He and Jenny had contemplated a place at the beach or the mountains, decided the beach was more for the children. The house was built by a combination of locals and some of his own Fearrington builders.

He keeps a low profile in politics. Registered as an unaffiliated voter, he has contributed to Republicans including former U.S. representative Renee Elmers, former U.S. senators Richard Burr and Elizabeth Dole, all of North Carolina, former senator Rob Portman of Ohio, and former Charlotte mayor and gubernatorial candidate Richard Vinroot. He admired the late Kansas senator Robert Dole, Republican presidential candidate in 1996. He has supported Democrats including former North Carolina governors Jim Hunt and Bev Perdue, former U.S. representative David Price, former state senator Howard Lee and Luther Hodges, when Hodges ran for U.S. Senate in

## Fearrington

1978, according to records of the Federal Election Commission and the state board of elections. Total contributions listed for him and Jenny Fitch for state and federal elections over more than 40 years come to just over $38,000.

He considers himself a conservative in that he prefers limited government intrusion on business activities. "Most small-business people are conservative," he said. But his conservatism didn't go so far as to support the late senator Jesse Helms or Donald Trump.

He is a strong supporter of WUNC, the National Public Radio affiliate. For the past 30 to 40 years Fitch has sponsored a brunch every January at the Fearrington House for donors to the station. WUNC personnel served as the waitstaff at the event for several years. Now the brunch, suspended for two years during Covid, is likely to have a speaker from the station or National Public Radio.

"It's a beloved event," said Regina Yeager, development director at WUNC. "R.B. has also done a ton of wine dinners for us, book readings, too. He has raised well over a million dollars, if not two million, for the station over the years."

He supports it because it is "a great instrument," Fitch said. "It's calm, no advertising. It's peaceful. It sets a good tone for the area."

Fitch also has served on the board of trustees for the North Carolina Nature Conservancy and the North Carolina Botanical Garden Foundation.

As a boss, Fitch considers himself "not a boss. I'm more of a coach." He can be gentle but firm with his orders. Doug Zabor said Fitch could sometimes be blunt because he knew what he wanted. Fitch said he prefers to give people leeway and to try to guide them rather than dictate.

"He gave you the free rein to explore what you could do with the job," said Phillip Cheeseman, who worked 10 years for Fitch, rising from waiter at the Fearrington House Restaurant to running the restaurant at the Granary, which was more casual and less expensive than the Fearrington House.

Working for Fitch was a pleasure, said Paula de Pano, former wine director at Fearrington House who now runs her own wine store in Chapel Hill.

## Two. Family and Leadership

Employees and former employees said he doesn't get angry. "His words of criticism were 'It's working or not working,'" Cheeseman said. "I've seen him frustrated, but I've never seen him mad. I've seen him sad."

Daughter Keebe, who presumably was subject to parental discipline at some point in her life, agreed he doesn't get mad. "I get angry for him," she joked.

"R.B. understands that every day you have challenges and difficulties and [you] treat them as 'Okay, how can I solve it?' rather than 'How can I get mad?'" said Gerald Bell, a former professor at the Harvard and UNC business schools, founder and chief executive officer of the Bell Leadership Institute in Chapel Hill and author of books about leadership.

As a manager Fitch "listened, just listened," Cheeseman said, and in that way he taught Cheeseman how he wanted to be as a manager. He learned that "if you listened long enough you answered your own questions." Cheeseman is now hospitality services director at a continuing care residential community in Raleigh.

"I've been very fortunate in having some very talented people work here, and they're very good at what they do," Fitch said. "And, actually, they're better at what they do than I could do, so I just figure I don't need to be there telling them what to do."

Laura Morgan, general manager for construction and real estate at Fitch Creations, which builds, sells and resells Fearrington homes, said Fitch is "gracious and he's kind, and he's tolerant of mistakes," she said, "but don't ever lie or tell him something that's not true. That's the one thing he asked, that 'everybody tell me the truth. If you tell me the truth, we can deal with it.'"

Fitch used to interview virtually every new hire, from dishwashers on up. He sought open, creative, friendly people. And people with a sense of humor.

"R.B. has always he had an excellent radar for good people," said Fitch's longtime landscape architect Dan Sears. "Everybody that he's hired it seems like has just been fantastic. I was grandfathered in, so I'm not a mark against his judgment."

Fitch said that for years he never had an application form "until the government says you got to have it to protect yourself." Ginny Gregory, former horticulturist at Fearrington, remembered that at her job interview she asked R.B. for a job description. "Really?" R.B. asked. At that, she said, "he grabbed a used envelope and a pencil, and he started writing down what my job description was."

He said he preferred to look at the work ethic and attitude of people, "did people take pride in their work, did they really enjoy what they were doing, did they have a sense of humor."

Laura Morgan said R.B. has become a father figure to her. "Working for him has kept me here, rather than exploring opportunities elsewhere and possibly earn more money. I didn't want to leave what he had created," she said. Plus, "I've seen him bend over backwards to treat his employees fairly."

Laura Morgan, general manager for construction and real estate at Fitch Creations, with her dog Luna (Fitch Creations).

Phillip Cheeseman said he was treated more than fairly. One summer he missed an entire month of work when he developed cluster headaches. R.B. was concerned, and he called him. "'Come see my massage therapist,' he said." Cheeseman took the massages at Fitch's home for almost six months. "He never charged me."

Ginny Gregory's furnace broke at one point, and her partner was ill, so for a year and half she had been heating her house by herself

## Two. Family and Leadership

with a wood stove. She asked Robert Flynn, Fitch's project manager, if he could install a furnace for her and let her pay him over time. Three or four days later Flynn, who met with R.B. almost every day, told her she would get her furnace free of charge from R.B. "Just consider it a bonus," he said. Gregory went to R.B. to thank him and said, "'I'm just speechless. I don't know what to say.' He said, 'Well, remember that when you come in here bitching about stuff.' What I realized was he really had a deep tenderness." The gift, she said, "changed my life."

Fitch has noted that a lot of his top people have been women. "Women are just very good about getting things done," he told the oral history project, wondering how many men would someday be reading it.

When Covid hit in 2020, Fitch didn't lay off anyone, and he offered employees $300 each to get vaccinated. The village closed for two months, and people were paid their normal wages, Fitch said. Fitch secured a Paycheck Protection Program loan to help keep operations normal, "so we didn't lose a beat," he said. The pandemic did bring a shift in hours that the stores, inn, and restaurant were open. Instead of Tuesday through Sunday the stores are now open Wednesday through Sunday, while the inn and restaurant operate Thursdays through Sunday. Those new hours have worked out well, said Greg Fitch.

R.B. Fitch wants an environment where people like coming to work. "If they don't like to come to work they're not going to be able to serve the customer worth a hoot," he said.

One result has been stability in his top staff. Morgan, who started as a bartender at the restaurant, has been with Fitch for 37 years, Theresa Chiettini for 24 years. Gilda McDaniel, director of weddings and special events, has been at Fearrington for more than 20 years, and Donna Mears of the gardening staff has been at the village for more than 30. All-around handy man and fixer Ken Henderson has been with Fitch for more than 30 years. Dan Sears, who retired in mid–2023, worked with Fitch for almost 50 years, architect Jon Condoret was on the payroll for almost 30 years before he died in 2010, and Robert Flynn was with him for 45 years.

# Fearrington

Gerald Bell said many effective leaders tend to have had healthy childhoods where they were loved and nurtured. That would seem to apply to R.B. Fitch. "I was the most catered-for child you have ever seen," he said. "I mean, I was picked up at lunch every day from school." His mother also picked up his clutter for him, "so consequently, she's raised a son that just doesn't put stuff away."

"Growing up feeling loved you're able to then deliver love," Bell said. "And in business, it's more just caring about people and accepting people, and not being overly judgmental. You have what I call a wide acceptance zone. So you're more likely to accept all people no matter what age, color, religion, race. It's just a person."

R.B. has all the characteristics of a highly effective leader, Bell said. "The best leaders in the world tend to be modest, and R.B. is modest and humble," he said. Good leaders also don't like to have people brag about them or put them on center stage. The healthy personality "knows that he's not perfect, and he knows he'll make mistakes daily. And he knows other people are really good and high quality from a carpenter to a plumber to a surgeon; they're all good human beings in there. So he doesn't need to be better than others to feel good."

Also, "he's not afraid to fail, and he doesn't take it as a reflection that he's a worthless person." Instead, he is "able to laugh at his mess-ups, fix them, and then start the next day anew."

Fitch reveres the English village model and talks fondly of the old days when there was less bureaucracy, when he could build a house in days, not months.

"I had a one-page form that I'd fill out," he said. "I'd take it down to the bank, I'd give it to the banker, he'd approve it, and I could close the loan the next day. It was really simple."

"That's the beauty of being in a small business," he told *Gourmet* magazine in 1984. "I couldn't hack it in big business. If I decide to do something at lunch, I want it started right after lunch and finished by supper." That he likes quick action is believable. That he couldn't hack it in big business is debatable.

Yet Fitch is not a grumpy old man dwelling in the past. He was ahead of his time in working toward energy conservation, toward more efficient building methods and modern marketing.

## Two. Family and Leadership

R.B. is "a problem solver," said former Chatham planning director Keith Megginson, and sometimes county regulations were the problem. Fitch would work with him to solve problems as they arose. "He was good to work with," Megginson said.

"He's had a really unique perspective, having been in business for 60 years in a region that's seen tremendous growth," said son Greg. "The swing from Old South to kind of New South is very evident to him."

# Three

# Partnership

Sometimes people just hit it off, create great partnerships, fine collaborations. Fred Astaire and Ginger Rogers, the Beatles, Woodward and Bernstein. The development of Fearrington Village is the story of great partnerships. First was the meeting of minds of Jesse Fearrington, who wanted aspects of his dairy farm preserved, and Richard Bell, the son of an Englishman, who had the idea for an English-style village.

Then there was the team that shared that vision of an English village, R.B. and Jenny Fitch, architect Jon Condoret, and landscape architect Dan Sears. Their collaboration lasted years and made Fearrington Village what it is.

"R.B. and Jenny had this concept or thought, just a dream, if you will, and Dan and Jon got it," said Laura Morgan.

"R.B. would ask their advice and what they thought of something and then listen to them and then he would offer other ideas," said Gerald Bell. They then became deeply engaged, "so it became their project in addition to R.B.'s." This team "would have fun together and laugh a lot and tease each other a lot and joke about their mistakes."

Jenny wasn't involved with Fearrington initially, but knowing her decorating skills, R.B. asked her one day to decorate a house. "From then on we started working together," he said. "She was just a creative person. She looked good, she was stylish, loved to cook, loved to garden, loved wine, loved paintings, loved the nicer, softer things, and drug me along," R.B. said. "We were best friends. I don't believe we ever had an argument." That could be because R.B. tried to follow his father's advice. "Son," he told him, "it takes two to argue."

"My parents were rare birds," said their daughter Keebe. "They

## Three. Partnership

**R.B. and Jenny Fitch standing, and seated, from left, Dan Sears and Jon Condoret, ca. 1985, probably on a trip to England (Fitch Creations).**

were around each other 24/7, and I would still hear them giggling late into the evening."

While R.B. worked with Condoret and Dan Sears on the building, energetic Jenny threw herself into planning and working the gardens at Fearrington Village, supervising the restaurant that came along, the decorating and interior painting of the inn and houses.

"She was one of the most creative people I've ever known, an aesthete and a visionary," said friend Moreton Neal. "She and R.B., also a visionary and brilliant businessman, were a perfect team."

"There's a lot of ceilings and floors and places around Fearrington where she would do the artwork, the furniture in the inn," said Dan Sears. On one trip to England, the Fitches shipped two containers of goods back to North Carolina including 13,000 feet of Norwegian pine from an old house along the Thames River. Fitch used a metal detector to find nails in the wood before installing it in the inn. Some of the boards are still there.

# Fearrington

**Jenny Fitch, ca. 1984. Working with flowers was one of her favorite activities (Fitch Creations).**

"Mom was sewing a lot of the curtains and table skirts and upholstering beds and all kinds of stuff like that," said Keebe.

Jenny "was Martha Stewart before Martha Stewart was," said Chip Callaway, who worked for years with Jenny on the Fearrington gardens. She was a "renaissance woman," said Dan Sears.

Jenny sought nothing ostentatious but an atmosphere that would make guests "feel very comfortable while they're here," she said in a 1992 interview.

"She exuded that friendliness, that hospitality, that stopping and talking to people," Laura Morgan said. "I think hospitality was just

## Three. Partnership

kind of ingrained in the way she grew up." And there was her laugh, mentioned frequently by those who knew her best. "You could hear her laugh across the parking lot," said Ginny Gregory.

R.B. said "he was the business end, and she was the thing that kept people coming."

"She was super interested in plants and planting, and she taught herself how to do upholstery," said Keebe. "She would go to Printer's Alley [a fabric store in Raleigh], and she found places where she could buy discontinued fabrics on the cheap. So she started decorating. How she did it with three kids is pretty interesting, especially back then" in the 1960s.

Jenny also got interested in food, studying at the Cordon Bleu in Paris and joining a cooking group that over time included such notables as Bill and Moreton Neal, who eventually ran the downtown Chapel Hill restaurant Crook's Corner. But first they started La Residence in the Fearrington House. "The restaurant was downstairs and they lived upstairs, but they called it La Residence because they were living there," Keebe said.

Jenny was R.B.'s foil, said Ginny Gregory. "They were the perfect balance."

If you wanted something done, it was best to get Jenny to talk to R.B., Gregory said. The key was cocktail hour. "When she and R.B. had cocktail hour, whatever she was thinking about or dreaming about, that was her time to pitch it. She had a 10-minute elevator pitch, and she was good at it." By R.B.'s own admission, the restaurant, the gift shop, the gardens were her ideas. "Basically, I made all the decisions, the final say, but a lot of times I'd go on what she wanted to do," he said.

"Dad let her do what she wanted to do," said Keebe. "He was smart enough to do that. Fearrington would not be Fearrington without Mom. She was the garden. Dad had no interest in food until she started taking him traveling and cooking for him, and so she really shaped him as much as anything else."

Jenny's death from cancer in 1995 was a blow to R.B. "He tried everything he could do to save her in terms of all treatments and experiments," said Gerald Bell. "But it really did hit him hard, like anyone." Bell and other friends took him out to play golf to help him cope with his sadness, "but it took him a while."

Dan Sears, who grew up in Arkansas and North Carolina, learned landscape architecture at NC State University and worked for the Bell Design Group as R.B. Fitch and Richard Bell were working out the plans for Fearrington Village. "I was the guy in the back room, one of them," Sears recalled.

Richard Bell had studied in Rome, Asia, and Africa and worked on campus master plans for NC State University, Appalachian State University, and others. Among his other projects were the grounds and interior gardens of the North Carolina Legislative Building and master plans for Pilot Mountain and Stone Mountain state parks for the North Carolina State Parks. "He was a great influence on me," Sears said. "He had a very broad worldview and design worldview." (Richard Bell died in 2020 at age 91.)

Sears established his own design company in 1979 and has

**Dan Sears, longtime landscape architect for Fearrington Village. Doing the job right means "designing with nature, working with the existing topography, not against it," he said (Sears Design Group).**

## Three. Partnership

handled numerous projects in the state, including streetscape improvements in Raleigh around the capitol building. His firm has won local and national awards, and his projects have been written up in *Better Homes and Gardens, Southern Living* and *Restaurants and Hotel Design*. He worked with Fitch for almost 50 years designing the streets and the neighborhood layouts. Fearrington is his longest standing client.

"I went with him because I liked him," R.B. said. "He has a real sense of what we want to do here. He's a bright guy, and he does exceptionally good work, and he also has a good sense of humor."

Jon Condoret was a well-established, supremely talented architect in North Carolina when he began working for Fitch Creations. He and R.B. met in the 1970s while walking the track at the football stadium for a fitness program at Duke University. Much later, "I approached him about doing work for us," Fitch said.

Condoret was born in Algiers and schooled in Paris. In 1962, he and his wife Joany fled the revolution in Algeria to her parents' home in Durham. Jon (the pronunciation is with a soft J, as in the French Jean) got a job with Durham architect Archie Royal Davis and went out on his own in the early 1970s. He never lost his French accent, which took some native southerners back a bit, Joany

Architect Jon Condoret. R.B. Fitch said, "Working with Jon was one of my fondest life experiences" (photograph copyright Jon Condoret Archives).

## Fearrington

Condoret told *Durham Magazine* in an April 2013 article. "People may have been a little leery of him, but not when they got to know him."

He designed houses in a modernist style characterized by flat or low-pitched roofs, open floor plans, unusual geometric designs, clerestory windows, tall windows, lots of other windows, skylights, and sliding glass doors to let in outdoor light.

Some of his houses are reminiscent of Frank Lloyd Wright and the prairie style. Condoret said his favorite project was the house in Durham, North Carolina, he designed for Arthur Larson, former Eisenhower Administration official and Duke University law professor, with its slanted walls, multiple angles, large open spaces, and a plethora of windows.

"Ideas flowed out of him like breathing," said his daughter Arielle Schecter, now an architect in Chapel Hill. He could draw upside down to illustrate a point for clients sitting on the other side of the table.

Condoret had spent most of his career designing expensive houses in the 3,000- to 5,000-square-foot range, but he didn't like the business side of architecture, the bookkeeping and administrative details.

"All he wanted to do was design," Fitch said. "He didn't want to manage people. All he worried about was trying to make enough money to make a payroll. He couldn't have fun. I said, 'Jon, why don't you just come work for me?'"

"He had the gentle soul of an artist," said Schecter. After working part-time for Fitch, in 1981 he closed his architecture office and went to work full-time for Fitch, where he needed only to design and draw.

For Condoret it was "pure joy." R.B. was a "turmoil of ideas" with a positive, let's-try-it attitude, Condoret said in a Learning Channel episode of *Great Country Inns*. "For an architect or a designer to be able to have a client that would let you [have] that freedom, it's just wonderful."

"It was a good deal for him and Fitch," said George Smart, CEO of U.S. Modernist, a Durham-based organization that works to raise awareness of and preserve modernist homes.

## Three. Partnership

Fitch and Condoret were similar. Condoret lived on a farm in Siler City, surrounded by chickens, horses, cows, stray cats and dogs and even an emu named Boom Boom. Both men eschewed bombast. When Jon and Joany Condoret got married, a harmonica player was the only music at their wedding. They felt anything more would be ostentatious.

"R.B. and Dad just got on like a house on fire," said Schecter. "They were really like soulmates in a way." Both sought to incorporate more nature into a development, preserve trees, design parks, keep old buildings and renovate them.

Condoret took the modernist style "and put an everyman take on it," said Realtor Jaye Kreller, who has sold many Fearrington homes.

"Homes must feel good to the people who are going to live in them, and they must have interesting spaces and elements of surprise within the design as well," Condoret said. He and Fitch were willing to experiment. "For every house we build, we often do as many as six different versions to achieve the final product that we think will work," Condoret told a Fearrington newsletter. "Many of the concepts we have worked on have not been used yet. They're just simmering in a drawer waiting for the right moment."

"R.B. was an excellent client for my dad, and he really, really appreciated that man," Schecter said.

"Working with Jon was one of my fondest life experiences," Fitch said.

At first, it was very different for Condoret as he was now designing smaller, less expensive houses. But he relished the opportunity "to work with you in designing smaller but more livable houses with good proportionate kitchen space and ample storage. Quite a challenge," he wrote Fitch on joining his company in 1981. "I am concerned that fewer and fewer people can afford housing and can appreciate the fact that you are trying to keep the cost down by creative development."

The first house Condoret designed for Fitch was 49 Trestle Leaf in the first phase of the village, the Historic District. It didn't sell for a while, so every time they drove past it Condoret would hide his eyes, Fitch said with a laugh.

## Fearrington

"Dad really liked designing small houses," Schecter said. "He always felt a house shouldn't be more than 2000 square feet, but you know, most people want them bigger. So they end up being bigger."

"He always told me, 'You must give the client what they want,'" Schecter said. Customer service, giving people what they want, was also a credo for Fitch. "I think I enjoy pleasing people more than selling something," Fitch said.

The Fitch, Sears, Condoret team plan at first was to build small, affordable houses that would appeal to young teachers or medical students at UNC. They were building houses aimed at people "who couldn't afford Chapel Hill prices," said Kreller.

Condoret's modernist style was "new for maybe a development, but not new to modernism for North Carolina," said Schecter, who designs modernist homes herself. "There is a tradition of modernist architecture in North Carolina. It's got the third biggest concentration of modernist houses in the country" behind California and New York.

Jon Condoret at work. "Ideas flowed out of him like breathing" (photograph copyright Jon Condoret Archives).

# Three. Partnership

**49 Trestle Leaf, the first house Jon Condoret designed for Fitch (photograph by Bill Arthur).**

That's largely due to the influence of Henry Kamphoefner, founding dean of the College of Design at NC State University. He taught there for 24 years, brought in top architects and had a visitors' program that included Frank Lloyd Wright. He gave the school national prominence and placed it "on the leading edge of modernism," according to *North Carolina Architects & Builders*, a biographical dictionary. His mantra was "the development of an organic and indigenous architecture ... to meet the needs and conditions of the southern region."

For a time, Condoret kept to his modernist style, which is reflected in dozens of homes in the Historic District, a style of architecture not typical of most other subdivisions. That suited Fitch, who liked Condoret's "European sense of scale." They added spiral staircases to some of the houses. "You've got to put some pizzazz into it," Fitch said, to make the houses more distinctive. They kept as many trees as possible, even planting some, especially in the Camdens. "I like trees," Fitch said. Cutting too many trees, just levelling the land, may make construction cheaper, "but you end up with a product that's not very charming."

Later buyers have enlarged many of the early Condoret houses, but most have kept the architectural integrity of the homes, and the Historic District still offers distinctive architecture not found in many other places.

"Condoret was a genius," Sears said. "He was a very creative architect, a most honest architect, honest designer," he said. "I mean, he's very pure. He and R.B. were developing that kind of Chatham County vernacular that's, you know, you see it and you know it looks like somewhere in the south, somewhere in North Carolina, somewhere in Chatham County."

R.B. Fitch nourished the design team, Sears said. "He's the best client all of us ever had."

R.B., Jenny, Sears, and Condoret—and sometimes Sears and Condoret's wives—travelled to get ideas—to Savannah, Georgia, where R.B. was fascinated by the city plans of founder James Oglethorpe 300 years ago. They also went to Newport Beach and Huntington Beach, California; to Charleston, South Carolina; to London and Bath and villages in the Cotswolds in England.

Condoret would sketch the layout of the inns they visited, and in the evening in their rooms they would have some wine and assess what they had seen, what they liked and didn't like, how it would apply to the inn they planned at Fearrington.

One of their hotels had heated towel bars. "I really like heated towel bars," Fitch said. They are now a feature in the Fearrington Inn.

On a trip to Paris, Jenny fell in love with some concrete sheep, wanted to ship them back to North Carolina.

"My dad was like, 'I'm not paying to ship concrete from France,'" said Keebe Fitch. Back home they found an artist near Charlotte to make the sheep, which stand today in the open space called Jenny's Park or Camden Park between the East and West Camden neighborhoods. "Everyone thinks they're alive, but they're sculpted," Jenny once said. Often residents decorate the sheep appropriately for the season—an Easter bonnet on a sheep's head or a wreath around a neck.

## Three. Partnership

**Concrete sheep in Camden Park. "Everyone thinks they're alive," Jenny Fitch said (photograph by Bill Arthur).**

Some of the lambs have occasionally been stolen, probably by prankish teenagers, guesses Greg Fitch. But the adult versions are too heavy to be easily spirited away. (The village actually had real, live sheep before it had goats, but they grazed the grass so short the cows couldn't get enough, so R.B. donated them to Ferrum College in Virginia. The concrete sheep "eat very little grass," R.B. noted.)

The Fitch–Condoret–Sears partnership "had a great time together," R.B. said. Jon Condoret died in 2010 at his home in Fearrington. "In the 30-some years we knew each other, never a cross word was spoken," Fitch told *Durham Magazine* in a 2013 interview.

While R.B. and Jenny Fitch and Condoret and Sears provided the creativity and the plans, somebody had to get it all done. They turned to Robert Flynn, a 6-foot-7 former mattress factory worker who became Fitch's project manager, overseeing the development of the land, the sewer plant, even the cows.

"They'd go to Flynn and say, 'How do we make this work?' And

**Robert Flynn, longtime project manager for Fitch, pictured here about 1982. "He could solve any problem that came along," said R.B. Fitch (Fitch Creations).**

here was this man who was probably the most brilliant inventor of them all," said Ginny Gregory. "He organically had what people go to school for. He was an inventor." Given a problem, he'd go home, research the project and figure it out, she said.

"He could solve any problem that came along," Fitch said. Flynn died in 2012.

## Four

# Open for Business

It was early November 1976, and R.B. Fitch was finally ready to show off his homes at what he then called the Creeks of Fearrington. He invited the public to view "new concepts in country living" at three model homes, 12, 13, and 14 Matchwood, in the Historic District north of the village center.

"These *Limited Edition* contemporary designed homes are now available starting in the low 40's," an advertisement said. "Each home offers the privacy of a woods-surrounded lot." The houses featured "skylit kitchens with greenhouse windows, spiral staircases, hard-wood floors, vaulted ceilings plus other space and energy saving ideas."

He advertised mainly in the *Chapel Hill Weekly* and on local radio with spots he mostly wrote himself. The idea was country living, "but with some sophistication," said Doug Zabor, whose Chapel Hill advertising agency handled the publicity for Fitch. Zabor remembers thousands of people visiting during the open house period from November 7 to 21, "way over what we expected," even though Fearrington was considered far out in the country then.

At first, Fitch's plan for Fearrington was to build small, affordable houses that would appeal to young teachers or medical students at UNC or Duke, people in adjacent Orange, Durham, and Wake counties who wanted country living while still residing near their workplaces. He was essentially following the model of his development at Polk Landing.

Fitch had gotten into the home construction business gradually. After completing his Air Force service in 1958, he worked in his father's lumber yard but itched to do more. "I was looking for more ways we could use our material," he said.

# Fearrington

*American Wood Council Design for Better Living winner for 1976*

**...visit Fearrington during our initial opening in November.**

Set deep in the rolling countryside around the hundred year old Fearrington farm, these *Limited Edition* contemporary designed homes are now available starting in the low 40's. Each home offers the privacy of a woods-surrounded lot.

Come look through the three idea homes featuring skylit kitchens with greenhouse windows, spiral staircases, hard-wood floors, vaulted ceilings plus other space and energy saving ideas like the Fitch Energy Monitor.

Pick a lot, choose a *Limited Edition* contemporary design which suits your family, and set a "move-in" date during the November opening of the "Creeks of Fearrington" section.

Enjoy an afternoon in our part of the country...between the villages of Chapel Hill and Pittsboro on Highway 15-501.

*New Concepts in Country Living from Fitch Creations (919) 942-5107, Chapel Hill, N.C.*

**the Creeks of Fearrington**

OPEN HOUSE 1pm-6pm
November 7-21

Advertisement in the *Chapel Hill Newspaper* for the first Fearrington houses offered for sale.

## Four. Open for Business

While working at the lumber company Fitch was elected president of the Lumber Dealers Association of the Carolinas. At the time, the federal government had a program called 241 that was designed to help people buy their own homes. He decided lumber dealers should help foster this program, so he built a house, mainly to see how much it would cost him. He sold it for about $10,000 as he recalled and then wondered why other lumber dealers wouldn't start building houses as well. "Then the idea came to me. Why don't I continue doing this?"

People began coming to him with land. "We'd build a house on it, do a septic tank and do a well, and they'd have a house."

He started Fitch Creations and opened an office next to the lumber company to do home remodeling and additions. (Fitch Creations and Fitch Lumber are now two separate companies with the lumber company owned by R.B.'s cousins.)

For about two years, Fitch continued building individual houses in the area—Hillsborough, Chatham County and Durham County. But he was having trouble keeping up with his work crews because they would be spread all around. "I said, 'This is ridiculous,' so I said, 'I think what I need to do is have a subdivision where it's all happening in one place.'"

He bought land on Mann's Chapel Road in Chatham County and built his first subdivision with about 150 houses called Chatham. The houses were small. "You got to keep it simple," he said, "but all of them had three bedrooms, a bath and a half, kitchen open to the living room," even a carport if the buyer wanted one.

He was the developer and the builder, and he liked the control it gave him. "If you're just a developer, unless you've got really strict rules, you have all this money tied up, you sell some lots, the first guy goes in and builds a house and decides he's going to paint it purple. Well, all of a sudden he's destroyed the value of all the rest of your lots that you've spent all this money for."

Next, he moved on to Polk's Landing. He was breaking the norm, building houses that were architecturally different from most other homes in the area.

"I took the hall out of the house. I took wasted space out. I got a little contemporary" with irregular roof lines, vaulted ceilings, skylights and clerestory windows. He sketched ideas on paper and turned them over to designer Claire Sutton to refine them. Chatham County didn't require building permits at the time so the process was informal. "You didn't have to have a lot of real fine plans," he said.

Building homes in the '70s with the fuel crisis and soaring interest rates, Fitch strove for efficiency and economy. He prebuilt wall panels, roof trusses and floor panels off site and trucked them to the construction site.

"Panelization gives us better control over production and scheduling, allows us to get a house dried-in quicker and helps us cut waste and pilferage," Fitch said.

Concerned that "half of the energy use in this country is a waste," he triple-glazed windows, used a lot of insulation, a lot of caulking joints, even installed controlled flow shower heads and toilets. Each of the early houses had bins on the property for trash and recycling.

Fitch "was way ahead of his time" in striving to conserve energy and preserve the environment, Doug Zabor said.

Fitch built homes with 2-by-6 studs instead of 2-by-4. "I was overinsulating homes," he said. But his houses won the North Carolina Environmental Design Award four consecutive years.

For a time, he even sponsored a contest among Polk's Landing homeowners in which he paid the lowest monthly electric bill. He noticed that the bills varied even though the houses were identical. That meant "the actual usage of the person determines more than just about anything I can do to the house, so their habits have more to do with energy usage." The contests cost him $60 or $70 a month, but it was "the best money I ever spent for advertising," he said, and he was able to note that energy costs in his houses were lower than in a typical area apartment. "They started coming. They started coming."

He figured that if people had a better idea of what their energy habits were costing they could save money, so he devised the Fitch Energy Monitor. It was built by Laurence L. "Chucko" Funk for $100,

## Four. Open for Business

Fitch said. Fitch told Funk he wanted "an electric speedometer, one that measures the electricity in dollars and cents that you're spending in your house at any one moment." It had to measure in money "because people don't know kilowatts," Fitch said, and it was to have "instant feedback," so a homeowner turning off a light could see the reading drop.

"So he goes away and he comes back with this thing with wires everywhere, and I have to go out and hook these things around the wires coming into the house before the meter box. The damn thing works," Fitch said. Funk even rode his motorcycle to the patent office in Washington, D.C., to patent the device. Officials there said it was the best application they had seen from someone who wasn't a patent attorney, Fitch said. In the end, it never worked as well as he hoped, and the engineers kept tinkering with it, making it ever more expensive. Eventually he dropped it, but the non-functioning meters still exist in many Fearrington homes.

Polk's Landing "was truly a thing of economy," Zabor said. "That's where he really learned how to build a development."

Fitch continued his efforts toward conservation with Fearrington Village. He had built a couple of solar houses at Polk's Landing and tried some more at Fearrington. One house used 550 plastic milk jugs to store heat collected by solar panels.

"The problem with solar houses was figuring how to store the damn thing [the

The Fitch Energy Monitor, designed to tell homeowners how much energy they were using in real time (photograph by Bill Arthur).

heat]. You could heat in the daytime when the sun's out, not a problem. But storing it so it did it at night was something," Fitch said.

Solar technology wasn't as developed as it is now, and Fitch's solar houses "got to be a hard sell because they weren't very pretty, these solar panels," he said. "It did not catch on at all."

Those first houses were a mix—most built by Fitch crews on contract for buyers according to a set of basic plans drawn up by Fitch and Condoret, but he would build a few on speculation to keep his crews busy when contract orders slowed.

In the high interest rates of the late 1970s, Fitch was fighting a headwind. But "it wasn't a killer," he said, because buyers could deduct mortgage interest expenses from their taxes and "it didn't last forever."

He said from the start that he was in no hurry, aiming to build 20 to 25 houses a year. "You can't hurry if you're building a community, a lifestyle. That takes time," he said. So each neighborhood would be substantially completed before he'd move to the next one. Besides, "if I finished Fearrington, I'd have to worry about something else to do," Fitch said. "I wanted this to last me until I was 85 years old, and I wanted to have fun while I was doing it." In 2024, Fitch was 90 and still building.

A unique feature of Fearrington Village is "the orderly progression of development over time," said Mark Ashness. "R.B. did not accelerate and decelerate the project based upon market whims. There were certainly time periods where he could have tripled the volume of housing construction based upon market demand but elected not to. I am not aware of any other project that was developed at a controlled pace irrespective of economic conditions."

Fitch "quite clearly likes to make money," said friend Gerald Bell. "He could have been one of the largest real estate people in America, if not the world." Instead, he emphasized quality of life. "I always admired him for trading off the possibilities he had of growth and expansion for seeing really what counted and the good life and good work.... So he built the strategy of building up a village rather than building up 5,000 real estate developments. Nothing wrong with that, but really the healthier your personality, the more you balance your needs and interests and [decide] that too much money doesn't make you much happier, if at all."

That's what Fitch said he has done. "I don't care about making a lot of money in a hurry," he told the oral history program. "That's one reason I'm in no hurry at Fearrington. I could have built it out maybe much quicker, but I don't want to. I want to do 20 or 25 houses a year. I could go another 10 or 15 years nicely, have a good life, have fun, you know?" The most important thing, he said is "I wanted it like I wanted it."

Fitch stipulated that people who bought a lot had to build within two or three years. He wasn't interested in investors holding the land for speculation, though he could be flexible. U.S. Foreign Service officer Michael Cotter and his wife, Joanne, had bought a lot in Fearrington anticipating retirement. But when he was named ambassador to Turkmenistan, Cotter had to commit to a three-year tour. Fitch agreed to the delay.

Over time buyers had more leeway for customized homes, but Fitch still drew some lines: he eschewed brick, preferred wood. He put utilities underground. He disdained in-house vacuum systems. When Evy Barrow and her husband were designing their home with Fitch, he refused to install the pocket doors that Evy wanted. "Something would snag, then you have to take the whole damn thing down to fix it," Fitch explained. Evy pleaded, R.B. stood firm. But when Fitch handed the Barrows the final house plan, it included pocket doors. "I yielded," because people wanted them, Fitch said later.

Fitch also wanted custom designed kitchen cabinets like those he'd seen in Europe with no visible hinges or handles, which might clash with a resident's decor. Will Johnson, Fitch's director of purchasing, found a local cabinet maker who converted his operation to the European measuring system to make the cabinets.

At first, he didn't build garages, but many customers balked. One man told Fitch, "R.B., we'll give up the basement, we'll give up the garage, but we're not going to give up both of them." He began building garages. "Yankees have a tough time giving up their garages," said developer Eric Andrews.

Fitch had some other idiosyncrasies. He banned mailboxes. To

## Fearrington

him, too many mailboxes around the county were damaged, leaning, painted all different ways—not a good look. Instead, he set up mail kiosks, with the idea that residents would run into each other collecting their mail. In a way, he was foretelling the future. The United States Postal Service now requires central kiosks rather than individual mailboxes at new residential subdivisions.

Fitch banned for-sale signs.

"I don't want it to look like the whole neighborhood's for sale all the time," he said.

His philosophy was to give people a reason to come to Fearrington. "It may be the gardens, it may be the food, it may be the bookstore, but visually it's got to look good, and you've got to want to come. If you don't want to come then I'm not going to be there very long," he told the oral history project.

Unlike many other modern subdivisions, Fearrington is not a gated community. "I just never cared for them," Fitch said. Gates are "a little plutocratic," and Fearrington residents "are not a gated community clientele."

There's a practical reason as well. Most of Fearrington's roads are built to state standards so the state will take over their maintenance,

The kiosk where residents of the Camden townhomes get their mail, one of several such kiosks in Fearrington (photograph by Colin Doherty).

## Four. Open for Business

plow the streets when it snows. The state won't permit gates on its roads. Without state takeover the cost of maintaining the roads would raise homeowner dues to an "astronomical" level, he said.

Early on, prospective buyers received a loose-leaf notebook, *Fearrington. A Country Journal,* which attempted "to present the facts and figures and people and product exactly as you would find them if you joined us this very day," marketing director Daneen Nyimicz wrote in the foreword. It told people about the overall community, the restaurant, and stores; featured interviews with residents and details about how the houses are constructed and with what materials; and covered the Fitch Creations staff, plats and house plans, village amenities and more.

It outlined the covenants, generally standard for the time, but they still say the only pets allowed are dogs and cats. Fitch said later that shouldn't be taken too literally. He wasn't after parakeets or hamsters but did want to ban horses and donkeys and the like. The idea was just to "set a tone," he said. He also banned television antennas and satellite dishes, but the Federal Communications Commission in 1996 forbade most such restrictions.

As Fitch developed new neighborhoods, Nyimicz produced separate neighborhood booklets, pasting snapshots in scrapbook style

The cover of the loose-leaf notebook once given to new or prospective homeowners in Fearrington.

## Fearrington

of homes, interiors and exteriors, local residents and points of interest. Some residents would receive a "settling in" book. In all it was a painstaking attention to detail. Fitch also sent videos to buyers and prospective buyers. He advertised that property taxes in Chatham County were significantly lower than in next-door Orange County (Chapel Hill).

He had a "Build and Rent" program in which he would find tenants for people who wanted a Fearrington home but didn't plan to move in for a couple of years. And there is the reverse, the "Rent and Build" in which buyers rent a house in Fearrington while they built their dream house.

Early on, Fitch gave each new home buyer a bluebird house, saying the area had one of the largest bluebird populations in the country. He also gave buyers a year's membership in the North Carolina Botanical Garden in Chapel Hill.

Fitch would sometimes go to great lengths to nail down a sale.

Bill and Jill Wargin came to North Carolina in 1977 for Bill to take a job teaching at the UNC Eshelman School of Pharmacy. They were both in their 20s and "poor as church mice," Jill remembered.

They went to Fitch Lumber in Carrboro to get boards for the standard graduate student library shelf—boards on cinder block. Ducking into Fitch Creations next door they encountered R.B. Fitch.

The next thing they know Fitch has them in the back of his car "with a Coca-Cola in a glass bottle taking us out to Fearrington," Jill said. He took them to a brand new house, 41 Benchmark, and said, "I want you in this house."

But it was $44,000 and they didn't have the money. Bill was so new on the job he hadn't even been paid yet.

"That's okay," R.B. said. "I'll get you the down payment interest free. I'll get you the loan." Stunned, the couple didn't know what to think. "We went home, and we called our parents," who were skeptical of R.B.'s promises. They went back to R.B., who, true to his word, got them a bank loan and bought out the lease on the apartment they had just rented, even paying the pet deposit. For the house, he threw in a washer, dryer, refrigerator, and stove.

"Everything went through, and it was probably the best thing we ever did," Jill said. They stayed in Fearrington for 15 years.

## Four. Open for Business

Jane Marlow, who came to the village in 1979, remembers those early years fondly. There was no village yet, and the road running south past the silo was just dirt. But, she said, "my kids had the best childhood here because they could explore everywhere. They would ride their bikes forever." Marlow was still in the village in 2024.

Ed and Marva Price were other early buyers. They wanted a larger house but couldn't find what they wanted, or could afford, in Chapel Hill. They heard Fitch's advertisements on the radio and went to meet him. "You could choose your plan, and then your house would be built," Marva said. It was 1978, and Fearrington was way out in the country, with fewer than 70 houses at the time, Marva estimated. But it had its advantages. "Moving to Chatham was very exciting. We could get a house that we wanted for the income that we had," she said. They were still in Fearrington 46 years later.

For years, Fitch held teas for newcomers. And he tried to meet as many residents as possible. One big difference about Fearrington from other developments is that Fitch, his daughter Keebe, his sister, Anne, and senior Fitch Creations staffers Laura Morgan and Theresa Chiettini live in the village.

"I have never, ever heard of a community where the developer was still there 50 years later, still lives in the community, still is building houses," said Rose Krasnow, president in 2023 of the Fearrington Homeowners Association, former mayor of Rockville, Maryland, and a former urban planning official.

Living in Fearrington meant the family "had such a vested interest in it being done right because it was their backyard," said Keith Megginson.

Many developers wouldn't dream of living in their developments, said Eric Andrews. "You don't want to live in the neighborhood because you're going to be the go-to person every time there's new construction, there's mud on the road. You're going to get a call" for all sorts of complaints or concerns.

R.B. Fitch said it hasn't been a problem.

"Nobody ever knocked on my door. No one's ever called my home to complain about anything," he said. "We're a part of the

## Fearrington

community. We're pretty much invested, so we want it done right. Besides that, I think it's a nice place to live."

The build-out of houses in the Historic District would take 10 years and eventually comprise 285 single-family homes.

In 1979, Fitch built a "Solar Dream House" for *Better Homes and Gardens* magazine, designed by Condoret and decorated by Jenny Fitch. It became part of a string of awarded houses in *Better Homes and Gardens*, *Family Circle*, *Good Housekeeping*, and *Southern Living* magazine over the next three years.

Fitch had been advertising in local media, and selling homes to young doctors and academics was doing reasonably well, but he had trouble attracting slightly older people with school-age children who considered the Chatham County schools inferior to those in Chapel Hill, in Orange County, or in Wake County.

Over time, he noticed interest in Fearrington from older couples, retirees who weren't worried about the schools and were lured

57 Benchmark, selected by *Better Homes & Gardens* in January 1980 as a "Solar Idea House" for the '80s (photograph by Naomi Rosestone).

## Four. Open for Business

*Good Housekeeping* **March 1981 Energy Saving Dream House (photograph by Naomi Rosestone).**

to the area by the slower pace, greater open space and lower cost of living than places north and west. The median home value in Maryland in 1980 was $58,300, according to U.S. Census data. In New Jersey it was $60,200. In North Carolina it was $36,000. That meant that many of those Yankees could pay cash for a Fearrington house.

**Fearrington**

Fitch thought, "Maybe there's a market there."

Thus ensued his decision to advertise in national publications such as the *Wall Street Journal*, the *New York Times*, and *The New Yorker* magazine, especially *The New Yorker*. It changed everything.

# Five

# *The New Yorker*

Kirstine Lindemann had for a number of years been intrigued by a tiny ad in *The New Yorker* magazine showing a leaping cow with a flower in its mouth and suggesting "Retire to Fearrington," where there are "bluebirds, belted cows, and fascinating people of all ages."

Contemplating retirement from their jobs at the University of Indiana, she and her husband, George Malacinski, began looking in the Raleigh, Durham, Chapel Hill area where they had relatives. They didn't immediately find what they wanted, so George suggested, "Let's go over to Fearrington Village. We have this little advertisement."

Lindemann needed no persuasion. "It was the phrase 'fascinating people' and the picture of the cow that really had captured my imagination," she said. Driving into the village they saw "cows, a silo, fences," Malacinski said. It felt like a New England village, where he grew up. "I just had a nice feeling. First impressions mean a lot," he said. They moved into the village in 2019.

They aren't the only ones steered to Fearrington by the one-inch *New Yorker* ad, tucked into back pages of the magazine sporadically over the years 1983 to 2020.

The ad caught the eye of Anne Angers before she moved to Fearrington in 2003 from New Jersey.

"I just saw the cow, maybe the cow wasn't there, but it said 'bluebirds and hollyhocks.' I remember that so well, it stuck in my mind," she said. The cow represented the Belted Galloways that graze at the village's entrance. Fearringtonians call them "Belties."

Deepa Sanyal remembers seeing the ad sometime in the 1990s when she was living in Chicago. "I thought, how lucky the people are who could live there." She thought it was probably too expensive and

One of the one-inch *New Yorker* ads that drew buyers from around the country to Fearrington.

exclusive for her. Fifteen years later when she checked out the village, "it was beautiful, it wasn't exclusionary." She moved in in 2009.

These people are typical of the many who have moved into Fearrington Village over the years as Fitch sought to expand his market.

While Fitch had advertised in the *Wall Street Journal, Harper's Magazine, Gourmet,* and *Foreign Service Journal,* the *New Yorker* ad was a masterstroke. Through it, Fitch reached a nationwide, upper-middle class, well-educated and mostly older audience of people who might be considering retirement. About 80 percent of *The New Yorker*'s readership is outside of New York, according to data from mediamaxnetwork.com, a company that handles advertising for Conde Nast publications, including *The New Yorker*. (The magazine has a circulation of more than one million and actually has more circulation on the West Coast than in the New York City area.)

"The demographics of *The New Yorker* fit exactly with the people that I thought would be attracted to Fearrington," Fitch said. Plus, "they had the best little ads anywhere."

*The New Yorker* is well known for its fiction and articles on politics, business, foreign affairs, sports, and the arts, and for its cartoons. Fitch kept the ad to one inch because it was cheap and fit his philosophy that the bigger the ad, the worse the place would be. "I had a caricature of the cow from some previous work, and people like animals," he said in an email. "Most people just read the cartoons

## Five. The New Yorker

and the little ads, so it was a natural." He wrote the copy himself. He couldn't say much. "You can only fit so many words in a one-inch ad, and I like brevity." The words sometimes varied, but the cow was usually there.

The ad worked. Fitch remembers getting neatly-typed letters from *New Yorker* readers attaching their business cards and inquiring about Fearrington Village. Laura Morgan estimates that at one point it may have accounted for as much as 30 percent of sales, with buyers from all over the country.

"That worked really well for him and changed the demographics of the community," said Bill Wargin, a Fearrington resident from 1977 to 1992. The ad skewed the population older, although, as the ad said, Fearrington has always been open to people of any age.

Today the demographics for *New Yorker* subscribers and Fearrington residents are similar. Average annual household income for *New Yorker* subscribers in 2022 was $129,631, according to Mediamax. The mean 2020 household income in Fearrington Village was $117,791 according to U.S. Census data. The median age in Fearrington Village is 73 while some 48 percent of *New Yorker* readers are 55 and older, according to Mediamax.

In 2018, the National Center for Health Statistics said Fearrington Village residents had the longest life expectancy of any U.S. neighborhood, a hardly credible 97.5 years. Well, it is statistics, and that number must be what the *Washington Post* called "a quirk of the data."

Still, the median age in the Fearrington region was 65, "easily the highest of any of the longest-lived communities in the country," the *Post* said. "It suggests folks don't move there until they've survived the dangers faced by young and working-age people. If they were going to die early, they would have done it elsewhere and driven down the expectancy in that neighborhood instead." Chatham County ranks fifth highest among North Carolina's 100 counties in longevity, with a life expectancy of 80.5 years, according to the University of Wisconsin Population Health Institute county health rankings published in 2023. (First and second were adjacent Orange and Wake counties with 82.1 and 81.6, respectively.) The Wisconsin organization also listed Chatham as among the healthiest counties in the state—No. 10—as measured by several factors including behavior, environment, access to and quality of medical care, policies and programs.

"The design of where you live affects your health," said Joanna Frank, founder of the New York–based Center for Active Design, which has sponsored and collected research on how designed environments affect health. "Your ZIP code has become a better indicator of well-being than your genetic code," Frank said, according to *Bloomberg Businessweek*.

As the *New York Times* noted in a November 2022 article, "experts in geriatrics say that people in their 80s who are active, engaged and have a sense of purpose can remain productive and healthy—and that wisdom and experience are important factors to consider." Education, marriage and strong family ties are also elements contributing to longevity, the *Times* article said. Such factors fit many Fearrington residents, who have a plethora of clubs and social activities to engage them. And they are educated, and studies show that the more educated you are, the more likely you are to live longer.

Almost 80 percent of residents 25 and older in Fearrington have at least a bachelor's degree, while nearly 40 percent have a postgraduate or professional degree, according to census data. (While Fearrington Village isn't incorporated, the Census Bureau's American Community Survey covering 2008–2012 listed it as the most educated town in North Carolina.) For *The New Yorker*, 62 percent of subscribers have graduated from college, according to the magazine's media kit.

*The New Yorker* readers and others that Fearrington has attracted have affected North Carolina politics. For example, the politics of *New Yorker* subscribers and Fearrington residents are similar. The Pew Research Center found in 2014 that 77 percent of *The New Yorker*'s audience "hold left-of-center political values," with 52 percent of readers holding "consistently liberal" political values.

No one has directly surveyed Fearrington residents' political views, but election figures show similar leanings. In the West

## Five. The New Yorker

Williams precinct of Chatham County, where Fearrington residents vote, registered Democrats outnumbered Republicans 2,160 to 1,204 in 2024, although reflecting a national trend, the biggest cohort was 2,470 unaffiliated voters. Fearrington residents make up slightly more than half the registered voters in the precinct, and it has gone for every Democratic presidential candidate since 1976. Before that there was no Fearrington Village. But that's not much different than Chatham County as a whole, which has gone for every Democratic presidential candidate since 1976 except for 1984 when it went for Ronald Reagan's second term.

A vote on one non-partisan social issue in 2009, allowing sale of liquor-by-the-drink in the county, shows a socially liberal bent. While the county's western and more rural precincts opposed the measure, West Williams voted 1,012 to 83 in favor of it. Overall, the measure passed in the county 65 percent to 35 percent. Similarly, when North Carolina voted in 2012 on an amendment to the state constitution to ban same-sex marriage, West Williams opposed it 1,610 to 581. Statewide, the amendment passed, but it was later struck down by the courts.

Chatham County's liberal leaning isn't all due to *The New Yorker* or Fearrington voters. Like other Americans, North Carolinians are "sorting themselves more and more into like-minded communities," said Michael Bitzer, a professor of politics and history at Catawba College in North Carolina.

Chatham County, once a mostly agricultural and factory-based county, has changed over the years to a commuter county with its northeast precincts more urban, or at least suburban, than the western precincts, filled with people who work at nearby hospitals and universities, the University of North Carolina in Chapel Hill and Duke University in Durham. Some commute to Raleigh, 33 miles to the east. They tend to vote Democratic, reflecting the national trend of urban and suburban residents voting Democratic while more rural residents vote Republican.

Chatham voters are also like voters in North Carolina's Research Triangle area of Raleigh, Durham and Chapel Hill. Wake County, for example, home of the state capital Raleigh, hasn't voted for a

# Fearrington

Republican for president since George W. Bush in 2004. And Chatham County residents vote. The county had the highest turnout of any county in the state in the 2020 general election (84 percent), according to the state Board of Elections data. Fearrington's West Williams precinct had 87 percent turnout. Chatham County also had the state's highest voter turnout, 65.97 percent, in the 2022 elections. Turnout in West Williams was 75 percent.

Fearrington Village now (2024) has some 1,500 homes with about 2,700 residents living in a combination of single-family homes and townhomes. The affinity of Fearrington residents and *The New Yorker* continues. The magazine has 7,000 subscribers in the Raleigh–Durham area, which comprises Pittsboro and Fearrington's 27312 zip code, according to MediaMax, equaling Atlanta, but far exceeding the whole state of South Carolina with 4,000 and Charlotte with 2,000. The Pittsboro postmaster estimated that about half the *New Yorker* copies distributed in 27312 go to Fearrington Village.

From being one of the poorest counties in the state, Chatham is now among the top six in per capita and median household income, according to census data. It also is the county with the highest home prices in the state, with a median sale price of $638,000, according to the local news app Newsbreak from data provided in 2023 by real estate brokerage Redfin.

In 2022, SmartAsset, an online financial consulting service, listed Chatham County as the most charitable county in the state based on how much people donate as a percent of their income and the percent of residents who donate.

Fearrington residents come from many walks of life—doctors and professors and business people. Residents have included a retired general, an admiral, and two former U.S. ambassadors, among many other Foreign Service officers. Many of them have never owned a home before, as their careers have taken them to numerous different posts around the world. (It helps that North Carolina doesn't tax retirement income of many federal employees.) For a while, R.B. said, he had "a flurry of Episcopal priests. There must have been, at one time, ten of them here."

The residents come from all over the United States and several

*Five.* The New Yorker

foreign countries. Of the village's 2,700 residents, 91 percent were born out of state, according to the 2020 census. That's indicative of what's happened to the North Carolina population over the years. In 1970, 24 percent of North Carolina residents over age 18 weren't born in the state. In 2020 that figure almost doubled to 45.1 percent.

Fitch ran the *New Yorker* ads until 2020, and they are legendary in Fearrington. He said about 60 percent of sales still come from word of mouth, and he is now better off advertising online rather than in print.

"The internet took over everything," Laura Morgan said. "We spend a lot of energy and money on search engines, on the website, so that if someone Googles 'retire to North Carolina,' we come up. That's really important. We need to be in the one or two spot."

# Six

# Growth and Change

Iconic is an overused word these days, but the silo and the white-belted Galloway cows in the field at the entrance to Fearrington are the icons of the village, a comforting site to residents and visitors, preserving the feel of a farm, which was part of the deal, what everyone wanted, when Jesse Fearrington, Richard Bell, and R.B. Fitch negotiated Fitch's purchase in 1974.

R.B. Fitch discovered the Belted Galloway cows while reading a *National Geographic* magazine. "I've got to have one," he said. In 1983 he purchased a bull and five cows. They have become iconic symbols of Fearrington Village (Fitch Creations).

## Six. Growth and Change

But Fearrington Village, of course, isn't a farm. It is a residential community with a farm anchor that makes the place softer than your average subdivision, more visually appealing, more livable. The houses and nature are integrated with houses well off the road, tucked in among trees and bushes. Most residents say the attractiveness of the village is what they like best about their environment. Besides the tons of trees there are open spaces and walking trails and paths and gardens and ponds and Jenny's Park. There's no sense that every acre must have a house, a structure, that all space must be utilized. And it's quiet, especially the further east one goes in the community from route 15–501.

"Our plans are to keep all these vistas and fields open permanently," Fitch said. "It can be done by varying the densities on the land as it's developed."

At first, houses were kept apart because they were on septic

**Aerial shot of part of Fearrington Village looking southeast showing the village center, the Camdens townhomes, and Jenny's Park (Next Door Photos).**

# Fearrington

Houses nestled among the trees in the Historic District where Fitch built the first Fearrington homes (Next Door Photos).

Gnarly tree outside the Fearrington House (photograph by Colin Doherty).

## Six. Growth and Change

fields. But later that spacing was part of the plan. Many of the latest neighborhoods are more like standard residential developments. But for much of the village, houses are nestled among the trees, not separated with houses here and a clump of trees there. While buyers chose from a few different house plans, they could make adjustments so houses look different from each other. As do neighborhoods. The Fearrington Homeowners Association lists 24 different neighborhoods in the village. Most are single-family homes, but houses in the Countryhouse Closes or Weathersfield are two- or three-home attached housing. Homes in the Camdens neighborhoods are closely spaced, more urban.

The plan from the beginning was to make the different sections compact and complete, "to make all the communities be an identifiable neighborhood," Sears said. Some streets have houses only on one side. On Village Way, the main entry road to the village, houses don't directly front the road. Only one house in the entire village has a Village Way address.

Maintaining the rural ambiance of Fearrington means "designing with nature, working with the existing topography, not against it," said Dan Sears, "and saving the woods and the fields in substantial quantities to make a big visual impact, and save the stream-way buffers that protect our clean water sources. Not having homes along every roadway leaves us with trees and pastures to calm our psyches and show us natural systems as they cycle through the seasons."

At Fearrington, "there was never an idea about a showplace," Sears said. "It was always an idea about being open and free and appropriate." Sears also didn't want the place to look "designed." If a space is designed right "it sometimes means that you can't tell that a landscape architect's been on the job," Sears said. It's art. "That's what they hire you for."

Fearrington "doesn't feel planned, but it is planned," said Realtor Chris Culbreth. "It shows in your streets and your trees, how the community meanders, and there's curves, and there's established trees and landscaping. It feels evolved and not put in within three years, and that's a hard thing to do to make something feel like it evolved."

**Fearrington**

In Fearrington, "there's no McMansions," Sears said. "There's no competition for who's got the biggest house."

"Pretty moderate, reasonable people live here," Fitch said.

The single-family homes were not jammed together, giving many houses an acre or so of woods or a spacious lawn.

"Fitch's small country houses come off attractively due to landscape-blending exteriors, individual siting on wooded lots (houses are not in rows), preservation of landscape character, and overall tone," wrote a reporter for *Southern Living* in 1982.

One thing that Jon Condoret preached to Sears was "the more you can crowd things together, the better they are." At first blush it may seem contradictory that compactness creates more space. But "the beauty of keeping things compact is that there's land left over that can remain a visual amenity. The farmland at Fearrington is like a golf course to us; it is the visual element; it's the thing that changes every season," Sears said.

Another thing. Cul-de-sacs.

"R.B. had more cul-de-sacs than most people," said Chatham County Realtor Eric Andrews. Traffic planners are skeptical of cul-de-sacs because they inhibit traffic flow and tend to dump many cars on arterial roads. But Fearrington Village wasn't designed for traffic, but for people, Sears said. The inhibited traffic flow reduces noise, and cul-de-sacs also contribute to lower housing density. There are 64 of them in Fearrington by Dan Sears's count, with many houses positioned so that backyards look out on the land rather than a neighbor's back wall.

Several of them are called closes, such as Clynelish Close, the Knolls Close or Baneberry Close. Close means cul-de-sac and is a word Fitch picked up while traveling in England with Jenny. Many street signs there used the word. Curious, Fitch turned down one of the streets and found "it was a dead end." He adopted the word for Fearrington in keeping with the English village theme.

"People love living on cul-de-sacs. You don't have through traffic," Fitch said.

"A cul-de-sac gives you a feeling of a little bit more privacy," Andrews said.

## Six. Growth and Change

Condoret said each cul-de-sac was designed "first for sun tempering, then for privacy, and then for spacial sculpture." That meant getting sun into rooms during the day and then easing it off from the west or south later in the day when the temperatures tend to be higher, Sears explained. "You can temper the south sun by just extending the overhang," he said. "You don't have to go but about 34 inches and you've blocked the sun so it never hits the wall of the house in the summertime."

Spatial sculpturing is more vague, regarding the proportions of a house, the overall look. "It's the art of it, what makes it look right," Sears said.

While early houses were on septic, Fitch built a village sewage system in 1981–82 after he decided to build townhouses.

Eventually, Chatham County decided to get into the water business after the federal government offered loans to establish such systems. County voters approved a bond referendum supporting the system, but it needed a minimum number of taps. "So we in essence gave our water system to the county, and that qualified them to get federal money to put in a countywide water system," Fitch said. Governors Club also donated its water system, he said.

Part of planning a community involves naming the streets.

"It's about like naming a child, and as hard as naming a child," Fitch said. It's also important, he said, because it is so permanent. "It's got to feel right to us."

R.B. Fitch, probably sometime in the 1990s. He's not sure (Fitch Creations).

# Fearrington

Almost everybody at Fitch Creations got involved, Sears said. Some of the women in the real estate office were very creative, he said, and, of course, there was Jenny.

"We went through the records of Chatham County and found out which names were available, and we reserved those names," Sears said. "A lot of those original names were more about landscape features, Hollyhock, Turtle Run, Quail Run, Windlestraw," he said.

As construction continued, "R.B. said, 'Why don't we name them for counties in North Carolina?'" So there is Forsyth, Halifax, Richmond, Tyrell, for example. "We deliberately did not name any streets Fearrington," Sears said, and avoided adding "street" or "road" or "lane." "It's kind of redundant. It's extra information that you don't need." Besides, eliminating the add-on "reinforces the neighborhood. It's not just a street. It becomes the name of the neighborhood."

At Galloway Ridge, the continuing care residential community opened in the village in 2005, Fitch suggested keeping to the Scottish theme of the Galloway cows, so Speyside, Glenturret, and Clynelish Close are named for brands of single-malt Scotch whiskey. Fitch Creations still has a number of names reserved for future development.

Starting in the early 1980s Fitch built 188 attached townhomes immediately to the east of the Historic District on Beechmast designed to appeal to buyers who wanted less home maintenance and didn't mind close neighbors. Each building has two or three homes, with gray siding and white trim, each with a one-car garage. The look is different from the more eccentric Historic District. And the homes added features that buyers said they wanted: spacious master bedrooms, decks, pantries, powder rooms, linen closets, laundry rooms and larger walk-in closets.

Fitch was responding to the market, building larger, more luxurious, and more expensive homes—spiral staircases out, large closets in.

The Weathersfield townhouses, in the center of the development, now consisting of some 104 homes, were approved in 1988. They were designed to replicate the Beechmast townhomes, appealing to older people. Fitch's message to potential buyers: "You can sell your lawnmower."

## Six. Growth and Change

The different neighborhoods have different service groups with differing services and fees. Some take care of lawn and grounds maintenance, others cover exterior building maintenance, fire insurance and weekly trash pickup.

Essentially moving roughly clockwise over the acreage, Fitch added to Fearrington when he bought 134.5 heavily forested acres from James Gust and R.B. Williams on the eastern side of Fearrington Village to develop a new section to be called the Woods. This parcel was not in the area approved for the planned unit development and consists solely of single-family homes mostly on lots of 30,000 to 45,000 square feet (an acre is 43,560 square feet) on and around Spindlewood.

First opened in 1987, the Woods offered homes more upscale than the earlier houses, though many of the earlier homes have been expanded or upgraded by the owners. Designed by Jon Condoret, they are also more traditional than the Historic District, and buyers had several options for design and layout. At the time, Fitch envisioned the homes selling for $150,000 to $175,000.

Still, the target market was the same as for the other areas of Fearrington: "Retirees from the North, the East and the Midwest. They love it here," said a promotional brochure prepared by the Sears Design Group. In keeping with previous phases, all utilities, including phone and cable, were underground.

One of the biggest changes came in 1991 with the building of Camden Park, tightly packed townhouses built around a 17-acre central park with two ponds just south of the village center. Two sections, East Camden and West Camden, each have a pair of small open squares of about an acre each in the style that James Oglethorpe designed for Savannah, Georgia, almost 300 years before. It was the result of five years of research, Fitch said, in which his team visited Savannah, Charleston, the Newport Beach area of California, and villages in England and France to discover how those towns attained their charm and livability.

Savannah "has the best land plan in the country with its parks and hierarchy of streets," Sears said.

The houses are reminiscent of Charleston–style houses, with

## Fearrington

many front doors not facing the main street but a side street. Garages are tucked away in the back leaving the main streets open for parking by visitors, shoppers and park users. "This plan accommodates the automobile, but it reduces the impact of the auto by using the

**Townhomes in East Camden Park (photograph by Colin Doherty).**

**View of West Camden townhomes looking south with Galloway Ridge in the background (Next Door Photos).**

## Six. Growth and Change

Autumn trees in the Camdens (photo by Ed Lallo, Lallo Photography, www.LalloPhotography.com).

Yancey Square in the East Camden neighborhood, one of the squares based on the street design by James Oglethorpe for Savannah, Georgia, 300 years ago (Next Door Photos).

alley system typified by all early town plans," Fitch wrote the county planning board. "Garages and parking spaces (at least two per home) are located on these alleys. The main streets have parking lanes to accommodate visitors, park users, and shoppers."

Camden Park "takes a leap into the past with narrow streets on a grid, hidden garages, sidewalks, street-level windows, neighborhood parks and stores," wrote a reporter for the *News & Observer*.

It was a plan Fitch had long envisioned to provide a downtown to the village, which is a short walk from most of the Camden houses. Buyers could choose from among six plans for their home. The area has a third section, South Camden, just south of East Camden.

From the outside, the houses look small, but inside they are spacious. They were designed "to explode" to the eye when you walk in, Fitch said. Such close quarters aren't for everyone, and some area developers questioned the viability of the plan. But Fitch pre-sold six of the houses within two weeks of putting them on the market in April 1992, the *News & Observer* said.

"We like the village aspect of it," one buyer told the newspaper. "We have just come back from Europe and it's really an appealing idea to us. Everything is in walking distance." Eventually, the

**A gazebo in the Camdens (photograph by Colin Doherty).**

## Six. Growth and Change

Camdens totaled 233 homes. Today, Fitch said, Camden houses are rarely on the market for long when they come up for resale.

The Bush Creek neighborhood was added to the PUD in the 1990s. Its 160 homes south of the Woods are a combination of single-family homes and townhouses. The Knolls, south of Bush Creek, followed with small single-family lots. The homes in Millcroft and Montgomery came next. In 2011, the Henderson Place development at the southeastern edge of Fearrington was added to the village, built on property owned by the late attorney Wade Barber. Barber sought a road connection off South Langdon because his property was landlocked, and Fitch agreed. Fitch Creations did not build the houses, and Henderson Place is not part of the PUD, but residents are members of the Fearrington Homeowners Association and have their own neighborhood association.

Since 2002, Fitch and other Chatham County developers have paid an educational facilities impact fee of $3,500 per single family dwelling unit. Chatham is the only North Carolina county that charges such a fee, which is aimed at mitigating the costs to county taxpayers of a rising school population. In 2022, Fitch announced plans for a new neighborhood, Granville, to consist of 41 homes on 52 acres off of Millcroft immediately west of Halifax at the southern end of Fearrington.

As Fearrington Village approached its 20th anniversary in the 1990s, it had become significantly a retirement community, not officially, but de facto. As these retirees aged, their healthcare needs increased, forcing many to leave Fearrington for continuing care residential communities, or CCRCs.

"What has developed is people have moved here and shown a great interest in wanting to stay here," Fitch said. He decided that rather than build another commercial center, which was to have been south of Camden Park, he would build a CCRC called Galloway Ridge.

Another incentive for Galloway Ridge was Fitch's desire to have an indoor swimming pool for Fearrington. He talked with people at Duke who said such a facility would work better in conjunction with a CCRC. "I said I would be delighted to talk about that," Fitch recalled.

# Fearrington

The result was the Duke Center for Living at Galloway Ridge. The center has a gym with a pool, weights, exercise machines and, at Fitch's insistence, an elevated track so runners and equipment users don't interfere with each other. An architect he was dealing with said it couldn't be done. Fitch took the architect to the Chapel Hill YMCA and showed him the elevated track there. "I said do it."

Galloway Ridge is a combination of independent living, assisted living, and skilled nursing care. It has walking paths, a community garden, a salon and barber shop, a library, arts and crafts and woodworking studios, an auditorium, and four restaurants and pub. Residents can live in apartments in the main building or in nearby villas.

At first, Galloway was to have been a for-profit entity, and a group calling themselves the Ambassadors, comprising people from Chatham, Durham and Chapel Hill, formed to get it going. Fearrington resident Hugh Chapin was chosen board chairman, but, Fitch said, "they could not get the financing worked out." They then

**Aerial view of Galloway Ridge with the villas in the foreground and main building in background (Next Door Photos).**

## Six. Growth and Change

decided to set it up as a non-profit, but the Internal Revenue Service said their principles of organization didn't allow them to qualify as a non-profit. Undaunted, Chapin went to Washington, D.C., and met with the IRS for eight and a half hours.

"When he left that meeting we were a non-profit," said Galloway resident Gloria Wilkins. "This place would not be here if Hugh Chapin had not done that." Today, the auditorium at Galloway Ridge is named for Chapin, who died in 2011.

"We massaged it and massaged it," Fitch said. "It was like giving birth over a long period of time. There were a lot of elements to put together." But while Fitch participated in the planning of Galloway Ridge, he left the construction to others.

There is a large tract of some 15 acres in the middle of Fearrington between Weathersfield and Bush Creek that isn't owned by Fitch and isn't part of the PUD. The owners are very private and have not wished to sell, but Fitch negotiated with them to allay their concerns about his continuing development, for example, putting up fencing and trees to shield their property.

"I must say that if a development had to come close to me, I feel very fortunate that it is your Fearrington Village," Grace Penny, one of the outparcel owners wrote Fitch in 1998. "I have grown to appreciate the creativeness and environmental consciousness that your Fearrington Village has brought to our neck of Chatham."

The Fearrington Homeowners Association had originally been formed in 1976 but was essentially inactive until 1980 as the village then had enough residents to make it viable. But the association and village social groups had to meet in residents' homes or a little house behind the inn. In early 1989, Fitch offered two acres east of the village for a meeting house if two-thirds of lot owners agreed to accept the offer.

"This is a very generous gift on Mr. Fitch's part, and for a small investment of our own" to furnish it "we can have a very valuable addition to the spirit and physical plant of our community," the FHA Board of Directors wrote in a letter to homeowners. There wasn't much debate as 95 percent of lot owners approved the plan for what is now called The Gathering Place, the venue for FHA

# Fearrington

The Gathering Place, site for many meetings and events at Fearrington (photograph by Bill Arthur).

board meetings, club meetings and other convenings. Jon Condoret designed the building, and construction proceeded during 1989. Residents provided the flooring, kitchen cabinets and appliances, raising money for them from sale of stuffed toy Belties, Beltie license plates and the like. The building opened in February 1990 and was expanded in 1996. The name, The Gathering Place, was coined by then–FHA president John Wait, who, for lack of a better term, called it "the gathering place." R.B. Fitch liked "the ring" of it, so the name stuck.

In 2005 Fitch built another building behind The Gathering Place to house Fearrington Cares, the non-profit organization that provides volunteer rides, minor health care and other services for residents.

In 1989, Fitch also donated the Swim & Croquet Club to the FHA. While accepting these donations, the FHA also accepted the responsibility and costs of running and maintaining them. The Swim & Croquet Club requires a separate fee but is open to all residents who wish to join. The same goes for the tennis courts, built in 1975. The adjacent playground opened in 1978. In 1981, Fitch donated land

## Six. Growth and Change

at Windstone and Turtle Run as a recreation area, which today has a basketball half court.

The FHA is responsible for enforcing covenants while separate service groups handle requirements for certain individual communities, such as the Camdens. Residents of those communities pay separate, monthly fees, according to each set of covenants.

The FHA publishes a monthly newsletter and, of course, weighs in on many issues concerning the village, such as the 25-mile-an-hour speed limit, what to do about the numerous deer that float through the community, or maintaining the mail kiosks and playground next to the tennis courts.

The FHA board on at least one occasion took a stand on an issue outside Fearrington. Although Fearrington wouldn't exist had opponents of the PUD prevailed in the 1970s, the board in 2001 went on record opposing the development of the Briar Chapel neighborhood just a few miles to the north.

It's a not uncommon syndrome. As Chatham County commissioners chair Karen Howard said years later on a separate but related issue, "At some point, we were all those people whose arrival was challenged. We have seamlessly integrated into the landscape, so much so that some of us are now challenging new developments."

As traffic in the county increased, the state Department of Transportation decided to widen route 15–501 to four lanes from two, a project that began in the early 2000s and was completed in 2005. Along with that, Village Way was bent slightly southward to align the entrance to Fearrington with the road to the fire station across the highway.

## Fearrington Cares

One of the differentiating characteristics of Fearrington Village is Fearrington Cares, an active, organized, compassionate entity not usually found in your typical subdivision. It offers numerous free services, including rides, minor home repairs, nursing services, medical equipment loans such as wheelchairs and crutches, recommendations for plumbers, carpenters, electricians and the like, and even companionship to Fearrington residents.

Governed by a board of directors and staffed by an executive director and two part-time employees, it is a largely volunteer organization and is supported entirely by donations, not HOA fees. A portion of the annual budget, $195,522 in 2022, comes from the Arthur Carlsen Charitable Fund, established by a Fearrington resident who stipulated in a blind trust that Fearrington Cares would be a special beneficiary among Chatham County recipients.

The 501(c)3 organization got its start in the late 1980s when Fearrington Village began filling up with older couples, retirees who felt a bit isolated in what was then a very rural area. They formed the Stay Put for Now organization with the goal of helping people stay in their homes as long as possible. The group offered rides, help with minor home repairs or maintenance, companion care and respite for caregivers and help from volunteer nurses and doctors who were village residents. Dues, at first $25, were reduced to $10 and stayed there for several years.

In 1994, a group of residents determined there was a need for

**Fearrington Cares office (photograph by Bill Arthur).**

## Six. Growth and Change

more readily available nursing services, so they established the Home Care Connection and hired a part-time nurse. The nurse operated out of a resident's home until R.B. Fitch provided space in The Gathering Place.

In 2000 the two organizations merged to form Fearrington Cares, now with some 150 volunteers. Fearrington Cares is recognized as one of the few such organizations supported only by donations, according to Barbara Sullivan, national director of the Village to Village Network, a national organization of community groups dedicated to helping older adults to live healthy, independent lives within their communities. Fearrington Cares even was mentioned nationally in a *New York Times* article in March 2022.

In most cases, "there is no charge for anybody to use our services or attend our programs," said executive director Karen Metzguer, and services are available whether a resident has donated to the organization or not.

The fact that Fearrington Cares offers its services to residents whether or not they donate is unique, said Mandy Summerson, former president of Village to Village, now geriatric care manager for Homewatch Caregivers in Chapel Hill.

In 2003, Fearrington Cares needed more space, so Fitch turned over space in the village that was formerly occupied by a UNC medical clinic. In 2005 Fitch built a separate building for Fearrington Cares, designed by Jon Condoret, just to the west of The Gathering Place. Eventually, "we outgrew it," said Metzguer. Using its donated money, the organization spent $750,000 in 2019 to expand the building, opening the addition in 2020. It now contains offices, a conference room, a consultation room, a procedure room, an equipment room and a multipurpose room. Fearrington Cares leases the land from the Fearrington Homeowners Association for $1 a year.

Staffed from 9 a.m. to 1 p.m. Monday through Friday, Fearrington Cares also offers support groups, educational seminars, Medicare information, and movement classes. Metzguer, a registered nurse who retired in 2023, made home visits and offered a triage clinic where residents could make an appointment to have their blood pressure checked, receive first aid treatment, get advice about

## Fearrington

their medications or other related help. She also helped people, such as diabetics, learn to administer their own shots. Kim Schneider replaced Metzguer as executive in June 2023.

Fearrington Cares also sponsors blood drives and flu shot clinics and publishes a vendor list on its website for people looking for cleaning services, car repairs, pet care, and computer and other services.

For a fee, residents can come to a foot clinic offered twice a month by a licensed nurse and pedicurist, or they can hire home health care for shorter periods than the minimum four hours that typical commercial services offer. For $1 a minute people can obtain help in 15-minute segments. This helps stop people from compromising their health because they don't want to pay for more time than they actually need.

In 2019, before Covid rearranged the world, Fearrington Cares made 51 nurse home visits and handled 382 nurse visits at its office. It provided 644 rides, made 245 home repair visits, loaned out 148 pieces of equipment. Almost 2,700 people attended movement classes, while 1,336 participated in lectures.

Metzguer emphasized that for true emergencies people must call 911. And for services that Fearrington Cares does not provide, staffers are trained to help steer people to the right people or organizations. "We want to point people to what we believe would help them," Metzguer said.

To raise money, the organization in 2004 produced a cookbook, *Flavors of Fearrington*. The first printing of 2,000 sold out and 1,000 more were printed.

Before Covid, Fearrington Cares held community suppers as a way to build community feeling. In 2022 Metzguer began organizing a new program, Fearrington StoryCorps, in which trained volunteers interview people about their life experiences. The plan envisions staged readings and other activities as part of what she called "formalized neighboring" to help people not just feel comfortable volunteering but also to help them feel comfortable asking for help.

"If you put 100 people in a room and ask how many will volunteer to be a driver, 98 will raise hands, but if you ask how many are going to ask for help, only two will," Metzguer said. She calls

## Six. Growth and Change

it the John Wayne syndrome in which Americans are supposed to be tough, independent people who pull themselves up by their own bootstraps. But "we are not independent, we are interdependent," Metzguer said.

Pulling yourself up by your bootstraps "doesn't work if you don't have any bootstraps," she said. Fearrington Cares aims to be the bootstraps.

# Seven

# The Village, the Inn, and More

From the beginning there was to be a village. Fearrington was not going to be just houses and a community swimming pool like so many other developments.

Houses were first. "At the time I wanted a village center, but I didn't care about doing it myself," Fitch said. He didn't even own the land for the village. It was held by the real estate firm that had approached Fitch about developing Fearrington, but they weren't doing anything with it, so Fitch decided to buy it and in 1982 began creating the village, renovating the existing farm buildings for new uses but without drastically altering the farm.

"I felt it would be really stupid to do anything to it." Fitch said in a 2021 interview. "That's what it's all about, the house, the barn."

The idea was to create something "along the lines of a quaint New England village with lots of charm and activity," said the "Country Journal" notebook Fitch Creations gave to new residents at the time. "I didn't really want any big businesses out here, just sort of the things I'm comfortable with," Fitch said.

*Village* was the key word. Fearrington would not be as urban or commercial as the much larger Reston, Virginia. "I think chain stores are great in malls," R.B. said, but not in his village. Fearrington Village is subdued commercial. The venues are under the supervision of general manager Theresa Chietinni, who has been at Fearrington for 24 years. All are owned and controlled by Fitch Creations except for the Truist bank. "You can't control the guest experience if there's another vendor," Chiettini said.

From the start, Fitch built a new entry road, Village Way, which

## Seven. The Village, the Inn, and More

**Signpost in the village center. The venues are just steps away (photograph by Bill Arthur).**

at first ran only about a quarter mile to Creekwood, at the time the main street into Phase One of the residential development. Village Way was extended later. He closed the entry road from 15–501 that ran right in front of the Fearrington house. "I wanted the road away from the restaurant," Fitch said. Jenny Fitch instigated the construction of the Knot Garden to the left of the house in what had been a parking lot.

In the makeover, the Granary, expanded with new rooms, new windows and some paint, became the Market Café and Deli and now the Belted Goat. Fitch envisioned it as a place to get "groceries, fresh fruit and produce, homemade soups and baked goods from the Fearrington House." It might have a post office, "a good cup of coffee and the Sunday *New York Times*," according to a Fitch newsletter of January 1982. Fitch wanted the *New York Times* to add a bit of sophistication to what was a small store way out in the countryside, so he'd buy copies from the Carolina Inn in Chapel Hill and rack them in the café. "I paid retail and sold them for retail," he said.

The milking barn was converted into Pringle's Pottery, where potter Jim Pringle made and sold pottery. The milking barn eventually became the Dovecote and associated stores. The corncrib, with corn still stuck in the walls, was moved to where it is now as the shed for the Roost, where patrons can get wine, beer, and pizza on Thursdays and Fridays in the warm months of the year. The main barn became an events center for weddings, corporate events and other large parties, but for a time it still had a dirt floor.

An inn had early on been part of the plan, but it didn't come right away. There had also been talk of a school, a church, an amphitheater, a lawyer's office, a travel agent, and a farmer's market, some of which Fitch tried. He also opened a seafood market, but he soon learned that "fish don't last but about a day." He tried seafood three times, "and every time I [lost] $25,000," he said. Then he tried a hardware store in the granary, because he loves hardware stores. "If a nail doesn't sell this year, it would sell next year," he said. But that, too, was short-lived.

There have been "so many iterations of that building," said Laura Morgan. "I mean, we've done it all."

### Seven. The Village, the Inn, and More

**The Granary about 1975, when it was a granary and the road that ran in front of Fearrington House before it was closed (Fitch Creations).**

A lot of the village center businesses are marginally profitable at best, "but they set a tone," Fitch said. "They are sort of the icing on the cake." Fitch said he doesn't mind losing a little money on something if it's done really well, but he finally drew the line on dinner at the Granary, which for a time had a restaurant. He closed it in 2017, saying he was losing $15,000 to $20,000 a year on the place. It had a reasonably stocked bar and served burgers and meatloaf and salmon at lower prices than at the inn, which is truly a special events restaurant. He had struggled with it over the years, opening and closing it and opening and finally closing it again, to the great disappointment of many Fearringtonians.

"There was nobody there," said Laura Morgan. "You just can't keep pumping money in something that's not supported."

In 2024 the Granary building housed the Belted Goat, which

serves breakfast and lunch Wednesdays through Sundays and is a high-end delicatessen of sorts selling wine, jams, cheeses, cookies, t-shirts, soft drinks, and more. In September 2023, Fitch opened Galloway's in the building, a wine and beer bar with salads and snacks available from 5 to 8 p.m. Wednesday through Saturday during the fall and winter.

McIntyre's, the bookstore, was built, R.B. said, "because of my daughter Keebe's interest in books," and named after his mother, whose maiden name was McIntyre. His mother "was very proud of it." In 2024, *Southern Living* magazine listed McIntyre's among the 15 most beautiful places in North Carolina. Designed by Jon Condoret and Jenny Fitch and managed by Keebe Fitch, the store opened in April 1989 and is a beloved feature of life at Fearrington with well-attended readings by many prominent authors over the years, including Jimmy Carter, Lady Bird Johnson, Dan Quayle, Gloria

The Belted Goat today, once the Granary. Now it is a site for breakfast, lunch, drinks, and high-end deli items and sundries. It also has Galloway's, a wine and beer bar serving snack items and salads (photograph by Bill Arthur).

## Seven. The Village, the Inn, and More

**Book-reading rabbit outside McIntyre's bookstore created by North Carolina folk artist Josh Cote (photograph by Naomi Rosestone).**

Steinem, Diane Rehm, Sue Monk Kidd, Kwame Alexander, and Jo Nesbo.

Carter and Quayle came with Secret Service protection, and Carter must have had writer's cramp when he was done. He signed some 17 books a minute, Keebe said, to keep the line moving.

"It's a place writers love to be asked to read," said Dannye Romine Powell, a former book editor for the *Charlotte Observer* and an accomplished poet who has appeared at McIntyre's herself.

"It seems like at least once a month we have somebody come in and say, 'I bought a house here because of McIntyre's, or I moved to Chapel Hill because of McIntyre's.' And I'm like, dang, so we're not messing it up too badly," Keebe said.

In the era of Amazon and big box stores like Barnes & Noble when even Borders couldn't make it, an independent bookstore like McIntyre's might seem doomed, and the rumor is that R.B. subsidizes it.

# Fearrington

**The reading room at McIntyre's bookstore (photograph by Bill Arthur).**

"We have been breakeven for a while and actually have come out of Covid doing well," Keebe said. Residents appreciate the knowledgeable staff and are happy to support the store, which is open to anyone. McIntyre's is part of what appears to be a revival of independent bookstores in the United States. The *New York Times* reported in 2022 that more than 300 new independent bookstores sprouted across the United States in the past couple of years.

"There's very, very positive things about shopping local," Keebe said. "We have done book fairs. We support the schools, we give teacher discounts." The store donates books to firefighters to while away the hours in the stations. "We really try hard to be a part of the community, and we do all these events with authors," she said. "You just do the best you can. I think that there's a definite anti–Amazon sentiment out there, and then there are people who come up with an Amazon credit card to buy their books," she said with a laugh.

Talk of a school in the village faded fast. Fitch offered to sell land to the county for a school but the school board declined the offer. He

## Seven. The Village, the Inn, and More

never considered a church. "I don't do churches," he said. Picking one denomination might offend people of other faiths. Besides, he didn't want so much in the village that no one would ever need to leave.

"I think it's important that in addition to being a neighborhood, you ought to get involved in a bigger neighborhood," he said.

The village has had a UNC medical office and pharmacy, a travel agency, a florist, a blacksmith, a post office, a hair salon, a jewelry and gift store, among other things. Today (2024), in addition to the Belted Goat, the village has the Roost Beer Garden, McIntyre's, a Truist bank, a spa, a real estate office, and the Dovecote store for high-end clothing and accessories for women. Expanded over the years the building includes the Nest, which sells expensive home goods, and the Sprout, which sells children's clothing and toys and has a pet supplies section. Then there's the 32-room inn and Fearrington House Restaurant. The village center has evolved as a sort of campus supporting the events at the inn or barn.

People at the Roost, summer 2023. They can get beer, wine, and pizza and listen to music on Thursday and Friday evenings during the warm months (photograph by Bill Arthur).

**Fearrington**

Fitch got into the weddings and event business "by osmosis. It grew organically," R.B. said, after people began asking to have weddings at the barn. Fearrington handles one to two weddings or other events almost every week, though that slowed during the Covid pandemic in 2020–22, Chiettini said.

The barn, costing about $8,000 to rent, can handle crowds of about 300 people seated and 700 standing. There is a garden terrace adjacent to the Fearrington House, a mostly outdoor space, three meeting cottages behind the house and a meeting room in the restaurant. There's also a meeting room upstairs at McIntyre's. The Fearrington staff handles all the catering. If you want music you can hire your own band, though Chiettini's staff can help you find one if needed.

The inn has about 11–12 employees, the restaurant staff is 30–35 people. Five to six people staff the Dovecote with 10–12 people at the Belted Goat, five or six at McIntyre's and about 10 people at the spa. Overall, Fitch Creations employs about 150 people full-time and about 40 part- time.

As with home sales, word of mouth for village shops and events

**The Barn set up for an event (Fitch Creations).**

*Seven. The Village, the Inn, and More*

Entrance to the Barn, site of many weddings and other events at Fearrington (photograph by Naomi Rosestone).

Cottages behind the restaurant. They can be used for meetings or other small events (photograph by Naomi Rosestone).

### Fearrington

is the best advertising, Chiettini said, though Fitch Creations sends emails announcing events to residents and potential patrons as well. And while patrons come from all over, about 75 percent of guests come from within a 50-mile radius.

The inn and the restaurant were developed separately. The restaurant came first. Jenny Fitch and Moreton Neal had been part of a cooking group, and in 1975 the group traveled to Provence. "I believe [Jenny's] vision for the inn and restaurant was inspired by our week in a gorgeous countryside relais near Saint-Paul-de-Vence," Neal said.

"I don't think I would be in the restaurant business if it weren't for Jenny," R.B. said.

R.B. and Jenny decided that a fine southern restaurant should be a major feature of their country village.

"Our goal was to provide a dining experience that was not just eating a meal but encompassed exceptional local cuisine, gardens, ambience, art and so on," R.B. said. "The most remarkable dining experiences Jenny and I had occurred when all these things came

**Fearrington House, July 1957 (Jesse Fearrington, Jr., Collection).**

## Seven. The Village, the Inn, and More

Fearrington House, spring 2023 (photograph by Naomi Rosestone).

together." As much as possible it was to be like dining in someone's home. But R.B. and Jenny didn't know much about the restaurant business, "so we talked Bill and Moreton Neal into staffing it for us." The Neals moved into the house and therefore called the restaurant La Residence, which opened in 1976. "Every week for about the first year I would reimburse them for the payroll," Fitch said.

But there was a problem. "We wanted to be able to offer wine with our French menu, and Chatham remained a dry county," said Moreton Neal. Voters had rejected beer and wine sales by about 2–1 in a 1974 referendum.

"They were trying to sell really good food, and people would pick up a bottle of Gallo and bring it down here, and it was hard to get it to mesh," R.B. said. In 1978, the Neals moved the restaurant to Chapel Hill, where they could sell alcohol. Bill Neal later established Crook's Corner in Chapel Hill. (The story of how alcohol got to the village comes in Chapter Nine.)

Jenny Fitch then suggested that she and R.B. open a new

# Fearrington

**Fearrington House restaurant at night. The bar is in the foreground (photograph by Bill Arthur).**

restaurant at the house. First, they had to do extensive renovations on the building, which had been constructed in 1927. "Every pipe in it was bad, all the wiring was bad," Fitch said. They built a new kitchen and glassed-in porches while otherwise making as few changes as possible. The old living room with its fireplace, to the right as you enter the house, became a sitting room for the bar to the left, which had been the dining room.

On trips to Washington and Williamsburg, Jenny Fitch obtained large platters and some champagne flutes to be used for wedding receptions and private parties. "We purchased French tarragon for the herb garden and unusual shrubs and plants for the flower garden at the White Flower Farm in Litchfield, Connecticut," Jenny wrote in "The Nibbler," a Fearrington House newsletter.

The Fitches reopened a restaurant in the house in 1980 as the Fearrington House Restaurant, and it began its journey toward fame in which it would win status as a five-diamond restaurant with AAA

## Seven. The Village, the Inn, and More

and five-star rating with Forbes. A complete lunch, including beverage, was $3.95. Dinner, with beverage and dessert, served Monday through Thursday, was $6.95.

"What we wanted," R.B. told *Gourmet* magazine in 1984, "was one of the best restaurants in the South."

While Jenny had studied cooking at the Cordon Bleu, she had many other duties at Fearrington, and the Fitches began looking for a top chef.

"Somewhere we'd read that a great restaurant is built on a great personality—then, in through the door walks Edna," R.B. told *Gourmet*.

He was referring to Edna Lewis, called by one writer "perhaps the most influential Southern Black woman chef in history." Her cooking credentials were impeccable: author of a book, *The Taste of Country Cooking*; consultant for Dean & DeLuca's specialty food shops; helper in establishing the esteemed Café Nicholson in New York. The Fitches were introduced to her through a caterer friend in New York and worked on luring her to Fearrington.

"It was my second courtin'," R.B. told *Gourmet*. "She was a delightful lady." Edna Lewis came to the Fearrington House in 1983.

The wine room at the restaurant. It has some 5,000 bottles of about 1,450 different labels, according to *Wine Spectator* magazine (Fitch Creations).

## Fearrington

The granddaughter of an enslaved man, she grew up in rural Freeport, Virginia, near the Chesapeake Bay. Lewis infused the menu with her southern specialties: corn batter cakes, country sausage, fried apples, poached eggs with ham. She also brought her chocolate souffle, which she had created at Café Nicholson. It was "as light as a dandelion seed blowing in a high wind," wrote New York *Herald Tribune* food editor Clementine Paddleford.

Top chefs in high-class kitchens are like generals in the army, not to be trifled with, and Edna Lewis was no exception. Ginny Gregory remembers Jenny Fitch asking her one day, "Take these vases in

Chef Edna Lewis, called by one writer "perhaps the most influential Southern Black woman chef in history," with Jenny Fitch, around 1983 (Fitch Creations).

## Seven. The Village, the Inn, and More

and get Edna to run them through the dishwasher. And I said, 'Oh, no, I'm not doing it.'" Jenny didn't want to do it, either. "I have to have a relationship with her. You don't," Jenny said. So Ginny went to Edna who said, "I'm not doing dishes. I'm a chef." But Edna did teach Ginny how to run the dishwasher.

Lewis was in her late 60s when she came to Fearrington, and eventually Jenny Fitch felt Lewis needed help in the kitchen. She turned to cooking show host and author Nathalie Dupree, whose classes Jenny had taken in Atlanta. Dupree thought one of her students, Walter Royal, would be a good fit for Fearrington. Royal had bachelor's and master's degrees in psychology and worked in the mental health field but turned his interest to cooking.

At the time, "there weren't many young, educated African-Americans, male or female, deciding to be a chef," Dupree said. "This was before food TV. It didn't have any glamour." But Royal had passion for the job. "You had to be passionate to leave a sound profession" for the kitchen, she said.

She urged Royal to go work with Lewis, who not only had cooking skill but also valuable restaurant experience. "She could teach him things that I couldn't." At first, "he thought I was crazy," but Royal came to Fearrington House. Lewis left Fearrington by 1984, but her chocolate souffle, once featured on the cover of *Gourmet* magazine, remains on the menu at R.B. Fitch's direction. "That's my only request" of the chefs, he said. Otherwise, he leaves them alone.

In 1984, Ben and Karen Barker, graduates of the Culinary Institute of America in New York who did a stint at La Residence, came to the Fearrington House kitchen to work for the Fitches.

"To our incredible fortune as young cooks, they took us to France for their application interview with Relais & Chateaux," an exclusive organization of luxury establishments that offers top quality food, lodging and service to guests. With the Fitches, they toured places that inspired their vision, Ben Barker recalled. "Jenny determined where we would go; she was totally in tune to some of the most magnificent dining rooms. We were exposed to several of the pre-imminent examples of transcendent cooking in an era of excellence that formed a lot of my cooking identity and firmed the

## Fearrington

acknowledgement that I was nowhere in that league. Karen maybe, but not me. It was an amazing trip that resounds to this day."

They stayed until 1986, when they left to open the late, lamented Magnolia Grill in Durham. Walter Royal joined them there and stayed until he left to become executive chef at Raleigh's Angus Barn, where he remained until he died in May 2023.

A succession of talented chefs followed, including Corey Mattson, once featured on Discovery Channel's *Great Chefs of the South* series; Warren Stephens, who would cook with his cowboy hat on; and Englishmen Graham Fox and Colin Bedford. Bedford was featured on some *Good Morning America* segments and stayed for 16 years before deciding in 2022 to move out West. Paul Gagne, Bedford's sous chef, replaced him, vowing to continue the quality and tradition of the restaurant. "In both our main dining room and our bar, we intentionally evolve our menus with the seasons," he told *Chatham* magazine.

"You can lose a lot of money in the restaurant business, but it's fun, and it's the flagship of the village," R.B. said.

Sometime in the 1980s the Fitches stayed at The Point on Saranac Lake in New York, a luxury resort built by the Rockefeller family. There, the innkeeper told them about Relais & Chateaux. To qualify, resorts must be owner-occupied or owner-managed and have fewer than 100 rooms, Fitch said. Standards are based on "5Cs": Courtesy, Calm, Character, Charm, and Cuisine. Rooms must be well insulated against noise, and "bedding must be in perfect condition and the bed must not creak under any circumstances," under the rules. The restaurant must be calm, and "any noise from the kitchen or service is not acceptable." The wine list must include "a range of half-bottles." Joining the group immediately appealed to R.B. Fitch. "It is sort of like a Good Housekeeping Seal of Approval with the upscale traveler," and travel writers notice it, Fitch said. "I built the inn to get into Relais," he said. The inn is subject to visits from Relais incognito inspectors. Fitch said there were about seven members in North America when he joined. Today, there are 48 members in the United States.

The inn opened in 1986 at first with 14 rooms. Now it has 32

## Seven. The Village, the Inn, and More

**Where you check in for a stay at the Fearrington Inn, with the plaque denoting membership in the prestigious Relais & Chateaux (photograph by Naomi Rosestone).**

rooms, 16 immediately adjacent to the restaurant and the others spread through the village center. The rooms are individually decorated and are "like stepping into a toned-down Merchant Ivory film," said a reviewer for *Forbes Travel Guide*, though they have flat-screen televisions and modern electrical and computer plugs. They come with Kingsdown pillowtop featherbeds and 300-thread-count Egyptian cotton sheets. Gardens are steps away from the rooms with benches and chairs for guests to sip tea or a glass of wine.

Jenny Fitch's vision was that the inn and restaurant would be seen as one entity, and that's pretty much the fact. Fearrington residents commonly talk about going to the inn for drinks or a meal even though the restaurant and inn rooms are in separate buildings. There is a bar menu that offers excellent but less expensive meals than in the main dining room.

In 1992, *The Hideaway Report*, a newsletter for sophisticated

# Fearrington

A room at the inn, advertised as coming with Kingsdown pillowtop featherbeds and 300-thread-count Egyptian cotton sheets (Fitch Creations).

The patio off the Sun Room at the inn, for inn guests (photograph by Naomi Rosestone).

## Seven. The Village, the Inn, and More

Fearrington House from behind (photograph by Naomi Rosestone).

world travelers, called the inn "the most unique country inn" they had encountered. *U.S. News & World Report* ranked the Fearrington House Inn among the top 24 Relais & Chateaux hotels in the country in 2024. *Travel + Leisure Mgazine* listed the inn as among the 15 best resorts in the South in 2022, though its Relais & Chateaux rating slipped to 4.5 from 5.0 due to "some quirks," Fitch said.

For more than a decade, the Fearrington Inn was the only hotel in the Raleigh–Durham–Chapel Hill triangle with a five-diamond rating from AAA. Getting that upgrade from four diamonds took some doing. Fitch had to put televisions in every room. Previously the inn had been sharing three portable TVs for 14 rooms. The Fitches installed three-way bulbs and full-length mirrors and expanded the staff, adding a bellhop and a night manager. In 2007, the Umstead Hotel and Spa opened in nearby Cary, North Carolina, garnering the same AAA rating. R.B. Fitch didn't see it as serious competition. "That's a hotel, and we're more of an inn," he told the *Triangle Business Journal* in 2013. "We try to sell charm and relaxation; they target a little bit different market. I think it's a plus-plus for our market."

## The Animals

Early on, R.B. and Jenny knew they had to make Fearrington a destination, give people a reason to drive out into the country from Chapel Hill or Durham down a two-lane 15–501.

"The most brilliant thing they did was they got a living mascot"—cows, said Ginny Gregory, a former Fearrington horticulturist. More specifically, black cows with white around their middle.

**Belted Galloways in the pasture (Fitch Creations).**

## Seven. The Village, the Inn, and More

The Belted Galloway cows became the iconic emblem of Fearrington Village—appearing on coffee mugs, t-shirts, jackets and vests—and, of course, they were featured in the *New Yorker* ads.

R.B. had contemplated a golf course on the land, but decided animals were more in keeping with the farm's history. Besides, he said, "cows were easier than raking a sand trap all the time."

In the 1980s, "I was looking through *National Geographics*, and lo and behold there was an article in there about rare and minor breeds in the United States of animals, and there was this Belted Galloway cow, this black cow with a white stripe around it" on a farm in Virginia, Fitch said in a video marking the 10th anniversary of Galloway Ridge. The breed originated in the north shore region of Scotland, making them a hardy breed.

"I thought, 'Hmm, that's really something, so I've got to have one,'" Fitch said, so he called the man mentioned in the article. "He told me where to go, and I rode up to Virginia, found some, bought some. In '83 we started with six," a bull and five cows. The herd has had as many as 30 cows. In mid–2023 it was 11 cows, six calves and one bull.

There are also three donkeys, Mary Alice, Jasper, and Charlotte, whose job is to protect the cows from coyotes, foxes, even dogs. Jasper is too ornery to associate with the cows so is kept with only the bull.

About 20 years ago, Fitch added goats, Tennessee fainting goats. "I saw a goat, a picture of a goat, a belted goat. I said, 'Ah, got to have a belted goat,' and you can get a whole lot of goats in a hurry if you're not careful." The goats don't really faint. They have a genetic disorder, and when they are frightened their legs lock, causing them to fall over. Next, Fitch found some belted chickens, Wyandotte chickens, which, like the cattle and goats, are also black and white. The animals are under the care of Bob Strowd, or "Farmer Bob," who has been with Fitch for 24 years.

The restaurant uses eggs from the chickens, but otherwise the animals are pets, not food. (Although hay from the farm is used to feed the animals.) They are a popular attraction, and on any given day one is likely to see people, with children especially, lined along the fences watching the animals.

# Fearrington

The Fearrington goats, black and white like the cows (Fitch Creations).

Fearrington chickens. Chefs use their eggs in the restaurant (photograph by Naomi Rosestone).

## Seven. The Village, the Inn, and More

The chicken coop. Benches line the road for people to sit and watch the chickens and goats (photograph by Colin Doherty).

Turkeys on the Fearrington farm (photograph by Ed Lallo, Lallo Photography, www.LalloPhotography.com).

They are popular with residents, too. At a Fearrington community meeting in June 2022 to discuss future development at the village, Greg Fitch said there would be some reduction in the herd of cows to accommodate long-planned further development south of the village center. The audience applauded when he added that many animals would remain.

Of course, there are the wild animals: deer and squirrels abound, and raccoons, opossums, foxes, and sometimes coyotes.

Then there are the birds, plenty of birds: cardinals, bluebirds, finches, robins, wrens, doves, nuthatches, woodpeckers, hummingbirds, owls, hawks, blue jays, chickadees, goldfinches, an occasional scarlet tanager, and, of course, crows.

## *Trails, Trees and Rocks*

Wending their way through the forests and fields of Fearrington are several walking trails and gravel paths. They are a major aspect of life in Fearrington and a labor of love, as the trails are maintained by residents and the Fearrington Homeowners Association.

The major trail—by definition in Fearrington trails are dirt and paths are gravel—is the 1.1-mile Creekwood trail along the road of that name in the Historic District. Early residents began using the trail to walk their dogs, following trails made by deer. The late Henry Castner blazed the trail, clearing and raking, aided by Colette File

The Creekwood Trail, one of the trails in the village (photograph by Ed Lallo, Lallo Photography, www.LalloPhotography.com).

## Seven. The Village, the Inn, and More

Sculptures by Fearrington resident Forest Greenslade along the Creekwood Trail (photograph by Bill Arthur).

and other volunteers. Now called the Castner Creekwood Trail and marked by blue-tipped trail posts, the trail has steps and bridges, one named "Le Pont De Colette" for File, who is originally from Quebec, and another for Fitch. It also has benches, a labyrinth, and sculptures by Forrest Greenslade, a Fearrington resident. It is truly a walk in the woods among the

Another sculpture along the Creekwood Trail (photograph by Ed Lallo, Lallo Photography, www.Lallo Photography.com).

# Fearrington

Cardinal on the North Langdon Trail, one of 18 carvings on the trail by resident Maarten Simon Thomas (photograph by Bill Arthur).

trees, ferns and grasses, as is the quarter-mile North Langdon Trail, also blazed by Castner, with 18 signature bird carvings by Fearrington resident Maarten Simon Thomas. (To see all 18 you've got to look carefully.) Another trail, the South Camden Trail, runs between Camden South and the Millcroft Closes.

Originally forested, the land that is now Fearrington

Signpost marking entry point for the North Langdon Trail (photograph by Bill Arthur).

## Seven. The Village, the Inn, and More

became mostly farmland once white settlers came in the 1700s. What were once cotton fields in the Historic District have since reverted to forestland, meaning that many trees in Fearrington began reappearing about 100 years ago and some 50 to 60 years ago.

Hikers will meander through a wide variety of trees—sweet gum, tulip, poplar, sourwood, elm, black cherry, black walnut, oak, maple, ironwood, and scores of loblolly pines. Surveys show strong residential support for protecting the tree canopy. "The benefits of trees to our community and to the word at large are myriad," said a 2020 report by the FHA's Village Attractiveness and Renewal Team. "Ensuring the health and vitality of our trees should continue to be a high priority for the village and her residents."

More than two miles of gravel paths, maintained by Fitch Creations, run alongside Village Way and Millcroft and throughout Jenny's Park, enabling residents to safely walk through the village. There is also a path looping around a wetland habitat in Galloway Ridge.

Characters you'll meet on the Creekwood Trail (photograph by Bill Arthur).

# Fearrington

Redwing blackbird carving on the North Langdon Trail by Maarten Simon Thomas (photograph by Bill Arthur).

Deer among the many rocks in Fearrington. Deer and rocks are ubiquitous in Fearrington (photograph by Donald Lokuta).

## Seven. The Village, the Inn, and More

A community survey in early 2023 showed that 79 percent of village residents use the pathways and trails. They are so popular that almost half the respondents, 47 percent, said they'd like to see more paths and trails, while 41 percent said they want them improved. An earlier survey showed support for raising FHA dues for trail maintenance.

So important are the trails and pathways that the FHA named a Trail and Path Task Force in 2021 that produced, with typical Fearringtonian thoroughness, a 30-page report listing potential new path and trail extensions complete with priority for each proposal, its length, a rough estimate of cost and who would need to approve it, from the state Department of Transportation to local homeowners.

Finally, rocks. One cannot go far in Fearrington without seeing the piles of large rocks, boulders, really. The village lies on what geologists call the Fearrington Pluton, an area where eons ago volcanic activity melted rock which then crystallized, forming the granite boulders that dot the landscape.

# Eight

# Gardens and Friendships

Gardens are an integral part of Fearrington Village. They flow around the Belted Goat, the bookstore, the Roost, and spa. Gardens frame the restaurant and the inn. They add color and comfort to the village, and they were the creation of Jenny Fitch. She envisioned them, worked them, and assembled a coterie of the finest gardening minds in the United States and England to make Fearrington a center of gardening beauty and knowledge.

"Fearrington became synonymous with gardens," said Chip Callaway, a leading American garden designer who works on many of the Fearrington gardens. "Jenny's appearance on the scene with Fearrington was sort of a horticultural renaissance—going on the same time that the food renaissance was going on in North Carolina. There were interesting people doing interesting things in their kitchens and trying to combine kitchen gardening with flower gardening, and so while the Piedmont was coming into its own culturally, it was also coming into its own culinarily." Fearrington was "the epicenter," he said.

Jenny poured much of her energy and talent into designing rooms at the inn and menus at the restaurant, but the gardens were her "utter passion," Callaway said. "She had a very personal hand in the gardens," recalled Fearrington resident John Webster, remembering her "at the crack of dawn with spade in hand followed by [her dog] Bubba and the gardening staff as she led them toward one of her many projects."

As Jenny faced the inevitable with her terminal cancer, R.B. asked her how she would like to be remembered. Not surprisingly, she answered, "By a garden." Today, her legacy lives on at Jenny's Garden, just steps out of the sunroom at the inn, and in Jenny's Park between East and West Camden.

## Eight. Gardens and Friendships

More than designing the gardens, Jenny Fitch tended them. She began by planting hundreds of daffodils behind the restaurant. Keebe Fitch remembers her mother outside at 10 o'clock at night planting bulbs. Jenny wasn't afraid to get her hands dirty and she came by that naturally. Her mother had maintained a vegetable garden, so Jenny knew the value of fresh food. And she had a knack for flowers, which helped when the Fitches opened the Fearrington House Restaurant in 1980. She arranged flowers for the restaurant and for weddings. A friend remembers an instance when Jenny rushed up to hand a bride the bouquet just before she was to walk down the aisle.

Jenny kept copious notes of her plantings. Soon, "people started coming up to her and saying, 'Can we have a garden wedding?'" said her son, Greg.

Jenny acquired a partner for gardening in Ginny Gregory, who was growing flowers at her farm in adjacent Orange County, North Carolina. Jenny showed up at Gregory's farm in her Mercedes (R.B. emphasizes that it was a used Mercedes that he bought for $5,000) and fashionable clothes and jewelry one day in 1986 and asked Gregory to bring some flowers to Fearrington. Gregory asked, "Who are you again? And she said, 'My name's Jenny,' and I said, 'My name's Ginny.'"

"I'm not in her social class, and she's not in my social class," Gregory said. "I was a hippie in overalls with tie-dyed shirts and work boots. And here she was all dolled up in her jewelry and everything." But they started meeting every Tuesday afternoon to arrange and discuss flowers and talk. They became fast friends. "There was no class consciousness in Jenny Fitch's brain," Gregory said.

Many of their arrangements were for the restaurant and the inn and for weddings. In the *Fearrington House Cookbook* she wrote in 1987, Jenny included instructions for topiary to adorn an outdoor wedding, and the bride's bouquet, and a honeymoon basket. Together, Jenny and Ginny learned which flowers last, which ones don't. They learned why cut flowers from the garden don't last as long as florists' flowers. Florist flowers are hybrid varieties. "There are about eight or ten varieties that are never going to die after five days in a vase," Gregory said.

# Fearrington

**Jenny Fitch (left) and Ginny Gregory, circa 1986. To Gregory, "it was the renaissance of gardening" (Bob Donnan Photography).**

After they worked together for about a year, Jenny said to Ginny, "You've got to go to school. You're not dumb. You can do this. And then come back to us." So for two years Gregory attended Sandhills Community College in Southern Pines, known for its gardening courses, learned the art and science of gardening, and then became the Fearrington horticulturist.

Many others who became involved in planning and fostering the gardens also became friends.

Ryan Gainey, a renowned gardener from Atlanta who designed gardens for that city's wealthy, helped design Jenny's Garden, including the trellis that surrounds the garden on three sides. "They talked every Sunday," Gregory said. Gainey died in a fire at his home in Georgia in 2016.

Chip Callaway, however, is very much alive and operating from his headquarters in Greensboro. He grew up in Mount Airy, North Carolina, and always loved flowers and gardens, but he became a newspaper reporter after graduating from NC State University. He had an epiphany after interviewing a landscape architect.

## Eight. Gardens and Friendships

**Jenny's Garden. It's just steps outside the back of the main house (photograph by Naomi Rosestone).**

"I was like, 'Oh, my God, you can do this for a living?'"

He has been doing it very well for years, designing gardens all over the East Coast, including the Andy Griffith Museum in Mount Airy, the Sarah P. Duke Gardens at Duke University, and the JC Raulston Arboretum at NC State in Raleigh. At Fearrington, he designed Jenny's Park between East and West Camden.

The Fitches loved England, traveling there many times, and loved the concepts of the gardens in England, "a land fairly choked with green thumbs," as one writer put it. These concepts guided Jenny's thinking.

One influence was Sissinghurst, a famous English garden created by Harold Nicolson and Vita Sackville-West in Kent County in southeast England. It's famous for its different "rooms" or garden spaces—a rose garden, a white garden, a cottage garden, and more. Jenny never met Sackville-West, who died in 1962. But she did become friends with Rosemary Verey, an English author and gardener who designed gardens for Elton John and then-prince Charles. Jenny befriended Penelope Hobhouse, also English, and an author who specialized in garden rooms and designed many gardens, including an English cottage garden for former Apple chairman Steve Jobs. Also in Jenny's circle was Rosemary Alexander, founder of the English Gardening School at the Chelsea Physic Garden in London—which has been a garden since 1673.

Jenny "loved to pull together people of like minds," Callaway said. Verey and Hobhouse would come to symposia at Fearrington, which became gatherings of the "green cognoscenti," the "speaking destination for anything to do with flowers and gardening at the time." Lady Bird Johnson spoke and walked the gardens with Jenny, Gregory said. Jenny also drew in such people as Dr. JC Raulston, founder of the arboretum at NC State that bears his name; Michael Dirr, a professor at the University of Georgia, whose *Manual of Woody Landscape Plant* is "biblical" for gardeners; and William Lanier Hunt, who was instrumental in establishing the North Carolina Botanical Garden in Chapel Hill. These were "all the people who were cutting-edge horticulturists in the country, and the barn would be absolutely jammed with people coming to hear these things," Callaway said. For anyone knowing Jenny, it was "not three degrees of separation [among them], it was more like one."

Callaway credits Jenny Fitch with helping invigorate interest in horticulture in the Triangle area. With the Sarah P. Duke Gardens, the North Carolina Botanical Garden, and the JC Raulston Arboretum, "suddenly we had three world-class gardens within spitting distance of each other, none of which had the same mission," Callaway said.

"It was just such a creative, fabulous time," Gregory said. "It was the renaissance of gardening."

Jenny was full of ideas. She fostered the installation of the intricate, twisted-branch chandeliers in the barn, made in Amish country, and did large floral arrangements for the entrance to the restaurant. "We were both Energizer Bunnies, and she could wear me down," Gregory said, laughing. "I'm trying to get out of the parking lot" at the end of the day. "She'd say, 'I've got an idea.' And I'd think, 'Oh, damn, didn't get away quick enough.' She was just brilliant."

## Eight. Gardens and Friendships

"She'd go to a dried herb farm and come back and say, 'Okay, we're turning the flower shop into a dried herb room,'" Gregory said. "And I'd call Robert [Flynn] and say, 'Robert, she's got another idea.' [He'd say,] 'Lord, I don't have time for it.'"

Today, chefs grab ingredients from the herb garden a few steps outside the restaurant. There is a flower garden and flower shop where the staffers cut and arrange flowers for weddings and the restaurant. There is a potting area and a greenhouse.

To the left of the entrance to the restaurant, in what was once a parking lot, is a knot garden—a type of topiary, a symmetrical formal garden using hedges to simulate a knotted rope. Knot gardens are a feature of many English gardens and go back to the days of Elizabeth I and fascinated Jenny Fitch on her visits to England.

A garden surrounds the Belted Goat, with daylilies, redbud, Shasta daisies, and hollyhocks grown from seeds gathered at Monet's Garden in Giverny, France. Overall, there are more than 200 varieties

**The herb garden, just steps outside the restaurant. Chefs use the herbs in their cooking (photograph by Naomi Rosestone).**

# Fearrington

**The knot garden outside the restaurant. Such gardens are a feature of many English gardens and go back to the days of Elizabeth I (Fitch Creations).**

of flowers, trees, shrubs and vines in the village, according to a history of the village in *Flavors of Fearrington*, the cookbook produced by Fearrington Cares in 2000. For a time in Jenny's Garden, just steps outside the sunroom at the inn, there was a rose garden. The rose garden presented a problem, as it required constant care and spraying with chemicals—to the point where workers objected to the work as a health hazard. But another drawback was that deer kept eating all the rosebuds. The garden was converted for a while into a white garden, and now is a more eclectic garden with more color, presided over by gardener Wendy Moses.

Replicating English gardens was difficult because plants that thrive in England wouldn't always survive in North Carolina's hotter, more humid climate. "We would have to find lookalike plants, or similar plants and try to make them acclimate here," Gregory said.

For example, delphinium grows in many English gardens. "It's a beautiful blue, the most treasured color in the garden, because there's not much blue in the garden," Gregory said. "Delphinium is quite aristocratic. And it blooms very tall, lacey, beautiful, lush, just

## Eight. Gardens and Friendships

gorgeous. And it would grow, and then the heat would hit it and it would melt. So we discovered that the native version is larkspur."

The park between the Camdens was also a problem. Modeled after the work of Frederick Law Olmsted, the designer of New York's Central Park and 19th-century English landscape parks, it is open, hot and dry. Jenny preferred flowers there such as rhododendrons, camelias, snowball bushes, hydrangeas, and viburnum that did well in shade, scarce in the park. There was one major tree, Callaway said. "I said, 'You need water out here.'" So they regraded the land so drainage from the streets would flow into the park. Today, the park has a creek, two ponds, a wildflower meadow and a variety of trees.

"I told Jenny, before we can make a garden that you're going to be happy with, we're going to have to wait five years at least to get rid of this merciless heat out here," Callaway said. Fortunately, they had five or six good growing years for the plants to get established.

Benches by one of the ponds in the park in the Camdens, also called Jenny's Park (Next Door Photos).

## Fearrington

Sometimes the demand for flowers for the restaurant and weddings would exceed Fearrington's ability to provide. That's when Jenny would get resourceful.

"She just had no aversion to stopping in her Mercedes on the side of the road and just walking into people's fields and cutting things," Gregory said. Once Jenny spied some Queen Anne's Lace in a field, stopped the car, and told Ginny to cut some. They had buckets of water in the back of the car to put them in. Gregory worried that they might be in some farmer's field. "I took great pause because I know that farmers have guns."

"So Jenny said, 'Just leave the car running,' and cut the flowers herself. She had no compunction at all. Ditches along the side of the road. She's in there just cutting daylilies or digging up daylilies," Gregory said. "She called them ditch lilies."

Pilfering flowers is apparently endemic in the gardening business. Ryan Gainey described doing it himself in a documentary about his life, *The Well-Placed Weed: The Bountiful Garden of Ryan Gainey*.

"All over the world, gardeners do this," Gregory said. "They go into famous gardens and before you know it, they've left with things in their pockets and seed pods and cuttings and it's like being a kleptomaniac. They just can't help it." Callaway said he did the same with Jenny in Virginia where they both had second homes near each other. "We'd drive by an old farmstead that looked abandoned, get out of the car and go up and clip hydrangeas, take them back, start rooting gardens."

All the gardens require constant maintenance, the knot garden especially, as raggedness would spoil its look, so Fitch Creations has a staff of seven full-time gardeners year-round, plus part-timers and interns to keep things in order.

As any gardener knows, not everything works. "If 80 percent of what you put in the ground lives—win-win," Gregory said.

Sophisticated gardens like those at Fearrington are expensive. By themselves "plants are not profitable," Gregory said. "There's no cheap way to do it." But the gardens have worth beyond themselves, an added value to the ambience of the village.

"People get lured here to see the gardens and end up in the

## Eight. Gardens and Friendships

bookstore, end up in the restaurants, stay in the inn," Callaway said. Gardens change with the seasons, looking one way at Easter, another way at Halloween. Jenny Fitch "was brilliant at using the gardens and the food to bring people to their business here," he said.

Callaway fondly remembers his time with Jenny. "We could get together and talk until two-thirty, three o'clock in the morning and have to remind each other that we needed rest. We'd be exchanging recipes and talking about cookbooks and telling gossip about garden buddies we'd heard from. And Rosemary [Verey] was working for Elton John at the time, and so we had all this gossip." They would still get together as Jenny's cancer progressed.

"I'd come down from Greensboro and we'd sit out in their garden and have drinks, which she wasn't supposed to have. And we would smoke cigarettes, which neither of us was supposed to have." Both of them "misbehaving," but some of the happiest memories of his life, Callaway said.

As a show of affection for Jenny on her 50th birthday, Robert Flynn gathered 50 small bags of sand, hung them from the trellis in the rose garden and put a candle in each one. She could see them from her room at the inn, where she was living at the time.

Jenny Fitch suffered through two bouts of cancer over five or six years, but she wasn't given to self-pity. "She never complained," R.B. said. "She never cried. She never said, 'Oh woe is me.' All she said was 'Cancer is a terrible inconvenience.'" Jenny died August 30, 1995, at age 57, leaving Fearrington Village a legacy of fine dining, luxury lodging, carefully tended gardens, and a strong sense of community. "Jenny Fitch touched the lives of all of us in Fearrington," said John Webster.

# Nine

# Getting Booze to Fearrington
*Legislative Legerdemain*

A restaurant can serve excellent food without selling alcohol. Think of a Muslim establishment, for example. But for a restaurant with aspirations to be world class, lack of alcohol is like Sousa's "Stars and Stripes Forever" march without the piccolos—nice, but lacking the inspiring touch.

"To have a first-class restaurant you need to offer the full range of services," wine, beer and liquor-by-the-drink, R.B. Fitch said. "If you don't have it, you're at a disadvantage." While not everyone drinks or always wants a drink, "it's available if they want it." Of course, alcoholic beverage sales improve profits, which can allow an establishment to add higher quality food and service.

Chatham County was dry when R.B. and Jenny Fitch reopened the Fearrington House Restaurant in 1980. There weren't even any ABC stores in the county. Drinkers had to brown-bag—bring their own alcohol in a bag, place it under the table and pour their drinks with the soda or other setups provided by the restaurant. The menu even noted, "North Carolina law requires patrons to pour their own drinks."

"We couldn't touch the liquor," R.B. Fitch said.

The menu also noted that brown-bagging wasn't permitted before 1 p.m. on Sundays.

Chatham County had tried twice before to ease its alcohol laws, but a referendum to allow beer sales at restaurants failed in 1974. Six years later, county voters rejected beer sales at restaurants by 458 votes and wine sales by 380 votes.

But the demographics were changing, and in 1984 supporters of

## Nine. Getting Booze to Fearrington

alcohol sales, the "wets," tried again. This time voters approved beer sales 5,668 to 5,417. Wine sales failed by 15 votes—5,481 to 5,466. Voters rejected mixed drinks sales by a slender margin—5,571 to 5,541—but they approved ABC stores 5,918 to 5,234 and that automatically brought with it approval for the wine and beer sales regardless of the votes on wine and beer. (At first it appeared that mixed drinks had passed, but a canvas of the vote showed a mistake in one precinct overstated the pro–mixed-drink tally by 100 votes. After correction, mixed drinks failed.)

On June 7, 1984, the Fearrington House Restaurant, the Belted Goat and the Roost received permits to sell wine and beer, and chef Ben Barker at the restaurant drew up a wine list. Sales started June 18. That was an improvement for the restaurant's bottom line and appeal, and it eventually became known for its extensive wine list, some 5,000 bottles and 1,450 different labels, according to *Wine Spectator Magazine.*

Step one achieved. Getting permission to sell liquor by the drink was next. By then, Charlotte and other places were allowed to sell mixed drinks after the state legislature in 1978 approved local option votes on such sales. Fitch was at risk of losing business, conventions, and gatherings to those areas and of not achieving his goal of a top-notch restaurant.

He eventually got liquor-by-the-drink for the inn, and the scuttlebutt for years has been that he pulled some strings to get it done. He did, legally, but not without some legislative legerdemain. First, some history.

North Carolina began statewide prohibition on January 1, 1909. After national prohibition ended in the 1930s, the state legislature passed a measure establishing the basis for the current form of the alcoholic beverage control system, according to Michael Crowell, a former professor at the UNC Institute of Government whose expertise includes alcohol laws, in an article in the *Campbell University Law Review.* Beer and wine could be sold in local areas that approved it, but hard liquor could only be sold in county-run stores in counties where voters approved such stores. Any bill allowing the sale of mixed drinks statewide was considered unachievable.

**Fearrington**

In 1971, the legislature passed a measure authorizing a mixed drink vote in Mecklenburg County, and, shortly thereafter, Mecklenburg voters approved the sales. But the state supreme court considered the Mecklenburg measure to be a local act because it applied to one county, not the whole state, and the state constitution prohibits local laws that regulate trade, such as selling mixed drinks. The court voided the Mecklenburg election.

Then, in 1978, the legislature passed a statewide measure allowing cities and counties to vote on mixed drink sales, and many of them approved those sales. But in Chatham County, any referendum to get liquor-by-the-drink was likely to fail. What to do?

Fitch got together with Howard Lee, former mayor of Chapel Hill and then a state senator whose district included Chatham County. They teamed up with other lawmakers and restaurateurs and came up with a measure to create "special ABC areas" where liquor could be sold, in many cases without requiring a vote of county residents. The areas would have to meet certain criteria and be in counties that also met specific conditions. This would not be a local bill, the reasoning went, because it wouldn't mention any county by name and would apply to all counties that met the criteria.

The late blind jazz pianist George Shearing used to tell a joke about his CD sales at intermission of his concerts. "All proceeds go to the blind," he said, "just not very many of them." That was the situation with the special ABC areas. The law applied to any county that could qualify. How many could qualify? Not very many of them.

Thus, one provision said, among other things, that the special areas could be set up in a county where ABC stores had been established but mixed drink sales had not been approved. The county had to border a county that approved countywide sale of alcoholic beverages and had an international airport.

The special area itself had to contain "more than 500 contiguous acres made up of privately-owned land and land owned by an association or club that is exempt from income tax on its membership … has more than 200 members, was created for municipal and recreational purposes, and, for three or more years, has levied assessments or dues and provided municipal services."

## Nine. Getting Booze to Fearrington

Only restaurants and hotels or similar establishments could qualify for these mixed drink permits, and restaurants had to have inside seating for at least 36 people and derive at least 50 percent of gross receipts from food and nonalcoholic beverages (later reduced to 30 percent). Fitch had support from the Chatham County commissioners, who unanimously passed a resolution urging the General Assembly to approve the bill, saying Fitch's restaurants had outstanding service and reputations and "serve not only local, but national and international customers." The General Assembly passed the bill in 1995.

Then, what do you know, here's Chatham County, which allowed ABC stores in 1984 but hadn't approved mixed drink sales and was adjacent to Wake County with its Raleigh-Durham International Airport and which had approved the sale of alcoholic beverages. And Chatham County had a community called Fearrington Village, which had more than 500 residents and more than 500 contiguous acres of privately-owned land with a dues-levying homeowners association of more than 200 members that was exempt from income tax on its membership income. It also had the Fearrington House Inn and Restaurant that had inside seating for more than 36 people and derived at least 50 percent of gross receipts from food and nonalcoholic beverages.

All that was needed was for a majority of Fearrington Homeowners Association members to approve sale of mixed beverages. No one was up nights worrying about that. On November 12, 1995, association members voted 214 to 4 for mixed drinks. The association then appealed to the state ABC commission for approval of a special ABC area, listing how Fearrington met the criteria in the law. The commission issued the permit on December 12, 1995. Mixed drinks had come to the village. They also came to Governors Club and the Siler City Country Club.

(There are other examples in the law aimed at specific counties, cities or establishments. Several years later the legislature adopted a bill allowing special ABC areas in a "county that borders on the Atlantic Ocean and has a seaport supporting oceangoing vessels" and a population of at least 52,000 among other criteria. Carteret County and the Morehead City port, anyone?)

Fitch said he no longer remembers the details of the effort but said, "We tried to move within the rules. We didn't break the law." Lee, 88 in 2022, also said he didn't remember details, but added, "That sounds like something I would do. We were doing a lot of creative things to get around the dry counties." (Fitch was a supporter of Lee's campaigns, donating $5,500 over eight years from 1995 to 2002.)

Fitch said he did it because "it's stupid not to be able to sell liquor by the drink." Besides, he said, it's not as if a permit ignites a free-flowing orgy of booze. "It's highly regulated," with taxes to be paid, limits on brands available, where the alcohol must be purchased and a host of other rules to be followed.

The new law added some complications for the agents who enforced the alcoholic beverage laws at the ABC Commission. Because the law didn't name any counties, Crowell said, the commission drew up a chart showing which counties had the special ABC areas.

That was the situation until 2009, when Chatham voters approved liquor-by-the-drink countywide, 5,187 to 2,756, showing how the demographics of the county changed over the years. By then, Fearrington House had had mixed drinks for 14 years.

# Ten

# Problems, Threats, Tensions, Good Works

As fine a place to live as Fearrington is, it hasn't been without problems, tensions, disputes, even a threat to its existence.

People have argued about the village speed limit, set at 25 miles per hour after debate between those who feel higher speed is dangerous and not fitting for a country town and those who see it as too slow.

In 1982, residents had a sometimes heated debate over whether Fearrington should have one central location for post office boxes or separate locations in sections of the village as they were built. The issue was settled when the postal service said it would serve more than one location, and Fitch agreed to provide the kiosks.

Fitch, of course, isn't immune to criticism that he is slow to properly prune trees, paint fences, improve pathways, or provide sufficient amenities for a growing population. People have debated what to do about the deer population, a problem not peculiar to Fearrington. For now, the solution seems to be to let well enough alone.

As more older people moved into Fearrington, some generational tensions arose. Children exuberantly shouting and splashing bothered some seniors who wanted a quiet afternoon by the community swimming pool, remembers Jill Wargin. Some retirees mumble that too many younger families moving in will change the nature of the village.

There have been other, thornier issues.

## *North and South*

Some northerners who moved in were surprised to see vestiges of the Old South as late as the 1970s, such as signs at Smithfield,

## Fearrington

North Carolina, on the road to the state's beaches, proudly saying, "KKKK Welcomes you to Smithfield." (The fourth K stood for Knights.) At least one sign also said, "Help Fight Communism and intergration," misspelling integration. The signs didn't come down until 1977.

Jill Wargin had a teacher one day ask her if she knew who her son was playing with, meaning Black children. Wargin said she knew, that they'd been to her house. She didn't make an issue of it as she liked the teacher, and the teacher never said another word about it. Two women navigating a changing world.

Conversely, many southerners have been wary of the influence on the local culture and politics brought by the influx of people to Chatham County from the Northeast or West Coast "lured, as I was, by gentler rhythms, more space and lower cost of living," wrote *New York Times* columnist Frank Bruni. In 2023, one person complained on Facebook about the "infestation" of the region by Yankees. The precincts in northeast Chatham County, with Fearrington Village, Briar Chapel, and Governors Club, for example, are more progressive, urban and heavily populated than those to the south and west, which means they can dominate in elections, leading to complaints from people in the rural, more conservative areas that they lack representation. This urban-rural divide is nationwide and hardly applies only to Chatham County.

In 2019, as Chatham County debated whether the statue of a Confederate soldier in front of the county courthouse in Pittsboro should come down, many Fearrington residents favored removal, contending it honored rebellion against the U.S. government and support for slavery. Some long-time residents countered that the statue was a symbol of their heritage and didn't condone slavery. Calls for removal come "mostly from people who have moved here," one person complained to county commissioners, although many native North Carolinians also supported removal. One man suggested that newcomers to the county were "guests" who should "try to assimilate a little more and embrace the South." Nevertheless, county commissioners voted to remove the statue.

## Ten. Problems, Threats, Tensions, Good Works

## *The Granary: No Village Pub*

Fitch has always envisioned Fearrington as an English village, and a staple of an English village is the local pub. Fearrington doesn't have one, and its lack may be the number-one complaint of village residents. "A good, affordable restaurant/pub" was frequently mentioned in a March 2023 survey asking residents what new amenities they would like to see in the community. For a time, the Granary had been a restaurant serving dinner with a small but decent bar that stood in for a pub. Fitch closed it for lack of patronage, saying he had been losing $15,000 to $20,000 a year on the place.

"We've never been able to figure out dinner" at the Granary, said Keebe Fitch. R.B. is "not a never-say-never kind of guy, but he's never going to do dinner here," even though "we have a lot of people asking for it." R.B. contends that the bar at the Fearrington House Restaurant replaces the Granary bar. But that bar is small, and the drinks and food are expensive. True, the bar menu is less expensive than at the main restaurant, and the food is excellent, especially the buttermilk fried chicken. But it's not a casual neighborhood bar. In September 2023, Fitch opened Galloway's, the wine and beer bar downstairs at the Goat.

"Popular demand was in part the reason," Fitch said, but "mainly we were looking for a place to go in the winter months when the Roost was closed."

Fitch has tried several different operations in the village. Many residents are not happy with the current arrangement, saying items in the Dovecote, for example, are too expensive and that the village center is geared more toward visitors attending weddings and other events in the village than toward residents.

## *Incorporation*

Worried about possible annexation by the nearby city of Chapel Hill, Fearrington residents twice considered whether they should incorporate to maintain more of their own control over the community. The first time was in 1990. Incorporation would have required the new town to provide services such as garbage pickup and police protection. To be able to receive state and federal funding, the incorporated area would have to levy a tax, estimated at as little as five cents per $100 valuation.

The debate produced "a disproportionate amount of animus and hostility between the pros and the cons, which continued too long," remembered Winston Kirby, a Fearrington Homeowners Association board member at the time. In the end, out of more than 400 votes cast, 87 percent rejected incorporation.

Fearrington resident Gene Moriarty spoke for many when he said, "There is no advantage to incorporation," adding that the village is "just as well the way it is now."

The issue arose again in 2004 and 2005 over the same annexation fears, though they were somewhat misguided because state law makes involuntary annexation difficult, especially across county lines. Once again, the issue drew much attention and debate. Higher taxes were again an issue, and R.B. Fitch wrote a letter opposing incorporation that influenced many residents. A report to residents concluded that the village wasn't likely to be annexed within the next five to ten years, that it could only happen with the support of county and state elected officials and that "incorporation is not all goodness and light." Residents rejected further consideration of incorporation 53 percent to 47 percent.

## *Wastewater Treatment*

In 2017, R.B. Fitch proposed to combine the Fearrington and Briar Chapel wastewater treatment plants. Briar Chapel would handle the treatment and then take advantage of Fitch's sizeable discharge permit into Jordan Lake. It would allow him to avoid costly expenditures to upgrade the Fearrington system, which was about 40 years old. Critics thought Fitch was selling the discharge capability at the expense of environmental safety. Others questioned whether the discharge into Jordan Lake was meeting state standards. The Briar Chapel system was seriously flawed, spilling more than 47,000 gallons of raw sewage since 2016, according to the North Carolina

Department of Environmental Quality. Briar Chapel residents produced videos of the sewage running along the surface through the development. You can imagine the kind of storm that ensued. The Fearrington Homeowners Association filed an objection with the state utilities commission.

"No money was involved," Fitch said. "I wasn't selling anything, I was giving them" access to his discharge permit.

"Little did I know" of the Briar Chapel problems at first, he said. He scrapped that plan. "We went back to ground zero," creating Fearrington Utilities, LLC, as a separate entity from Fitch Creations, and upgrading the system with work beginning in 2022 and completion expected in late summer 2024, though he warned that rates would have to rise. "All we want is basically a return on investment," he said.

## Highway Bypass: A Threat

In 1989, the N.C. Department of Transportation was looking for a bypass highway to route traffic from Pittsboro around Chapel Hill toward I-40, Durham, Raleigh, and the Research Triangle Park. The idea was to reduce traffic on 15–501, which at the time was a two-lane road. One proposed route would have bisected Fearrington Village, starting where Weathersfield and 15–501 meet and running northeast toward Lystra Road.

The route was "our best professional recommendation," highway planning engineer Blake Norwood said.

R.B. Fitch went to work rallying opposition to the road.

"Just when you think you can relax and enjoy the spring flowers," he wrote in a May 1989 letter to Fearrington residents, "someone with a grease pencil draws a line through Fearrington and says, 'Let's put a four-lane perimeter road here.' Unbelievable, but so."

Fearrington residents glared with disapproval when the DOT posted maps of the proposed route in the barn, envisioning thousands of cars moving through the area every day.

The bypass "would have ruined Fearrington," said Fitch, encouraging residents to write the governor, their state senators and representatives, the state transportation secretary, and members of the Chatham County Board of Commissioners. Fearringtonians and other residents in the area, not unskilled in lobbying government officials, were happy to do so.

The proposed road would pass through "the only developed neighborhood in this area," resident Carl Stromee wrote the chairman of the county commissioners. It would destroy 80 to 100 homes and threaten at least 50 more houses under construction, wrote Fearrington resident Will Heiser to the Chatham County manager. It looked like the road might also take out the Fearrington swimming pool. The FHA said the road would be a "serious safety hazard" and suggested widening of U.S. 15–501 instead.

Besides letters, Fearrington people presented a petition with 739 signatures opposing the road to county commissioners. Some 300 Fearrington residents showed up at a public hearing in Durham to object, according to the *Chapel Hill News*. We want "complete elimination" of any plans to build the bypass, one Fearrington resident said to resounding applause. The protesters "roasted" the highway officials, Fitch said. The DOT read the situation and dropped the plan. Instead, in the early 2000s, the department began widening 15–501 to four lanes, completing the job in 2005.

## *Hurricane Fran*

On September 5, 1996, Hurricane Fran slammed into North Carolina as a Category Three storm with winds up to 115 miles an hour. Making landfall near Wilmington at about 8:30 p.m., the storm slid up through central North Carolina, knocking down trees, damaging homes, killing the power, causing flooding. Fearrington Village was not exempt.

"It was the scariest night of my life," remembered Jeanne Riddle, who lived on Spindlewood at the time. She could hear thumping on her roof, trees crashing and limbs breaking. The power was out and she lay in bed in the dark "wondering when the next loblolly was going to crash through our window or the roof."

Evy Barrow remembers waking up at night and hearing a lot of

## Ten. Problems, Threats, Tensions, Good Works

noise. "Gosh, that sounds like trees falling in the forest," she thought. When she awoke the next morning and looked outside, she saw "it really was trees falling in the forest."

One house in the Historic District was completely crushed, but the woman who lived there got out safely, remembered Sally Earnest. Perhaps it was the same house that Ruth Moose remembered being destroyed, but she said the owner was in Europe. "If she had been in there that night she would have been killed," Moose said.

Moose and her husband had been in Albemarle when the storm hit. They were in the process of moving into their home on Matchwood and had left some outdoor furniture on the deck. "I just knew when we got back to Fearrington that deck furniture would be smashed all over the lot," but such were the idiosyncrasies of the storm that "it wasn't touched." A tree in their yard, however, fell into their nextdoor neighbor's dining room.

Trees were down all over the place. Marva Price, on Shagbark in the Historic District, remembered getting in her car the next morning. "A man stopped me and said, 'Where are you going?' I said, 'I'm

It's not Hurricane Fran, but it is a nighttime thunderstorm at Fearrington (photograph by Ed Lallo, Lallo Photography, www.LalloPhotography.com).

going to work.' He said, 'No, you're not, there are trees on the road.'" Turned out 50 trees were down on Price's property.

At Jeanne Riddle's house, water poured into her sunroom, and 21 trees were down in her backyard. "Along the entire back wall in the living room all I could see were loblolly branches. I couldn't see out of my windows." They had $10,000 worth of damage.

Power was out in the village, of course, which meant Fitch couldn't open the Market Place (now the Belted Goat). Not knowing how long the power would be out, the staff began giving away food to residents before it could spoil, said Laura Morgan. They probably didn't need to. Morgan remembered the power coming back on in mid- to late afternoon, and well before people in the surrounding areas got power back.

Then the cleanup came, as the village began taking care of its own. Residents with chainsaws cut away trees blocking the roads, said Marva Price. Fitch construction crews also went to work clearing the roads, cutting up trees and putting blue tarps over damaged houses, Jeanne Riddle remembered.

Lumber crews hired by Fitch went into people's yards to clear them and cut down remaining trees in danger of falling. Crews brought in a 100-foot crane to lift trees off Jeanne Riddle's house. Fitch didn't charge anyone for the service, remembered Moose, Price, and Riddle.

"We do what we need to do," R.B. Fitch said years later. "It was a mess. We spent about a year cleaning it up."

It could have been worse. In Raleigh, Crabtree Valley Mall stores were closed for weeks, some for months, because of flooding.

Overall, Fran caused 24 deaths in North Carolina, none in Fearrington; destroyed 8.2 million acres of forestland; and caused $5.2 billion worth of damage to the state. (In 2018, Hurricane Florence became the costliest natural disaster in North Carolina history, killing 53 people in the state, but its worst effects were felt mostly to the east of Chatham County.)

## *A Nice Thing*

In the summer of 1999, the international Special Olympics came to Raleigh, Durham, and Chapel Hill—and to Pittsboro, where the

## Ten. Problems, Threats, Tensions, Good Works

bocce competition was held at Fearrington on a field behind the Camden mail kiosk.

The event presented 19 different sports with some 7,000 participants from 150 different nations, according to Fearrington resident Robert Holton, who was among the leading volunteers. About 300 athletes and coaches participated in the bocce competition.

R.B. Fitch built 12 bocce courts and erected tents and stands for spectators and officials. Some 300 Fearrington residents volunteered to help sponsor the games. Game officials were housed in Fearrington guest rooms or even homes whose owners were out of town.

"The weather was very hot, and the committee had their hands full passing out water to make sure everyone was hydrated," Holton said.

Eunice Kennedy Shriver, president of the U.S. Special Olympics at the time, attended the bocce games. Ed Price, head of the Fearrington pool club, opened the pool to game officials, the Fearrington bocce committee and host families for a closing party.

"The participants and officials could not say enough about the kindness of the Fearrington residents and the great support they felt during the games," Holton said.

# Eleven

# The Future

R.B. Fitch said from the beginning that he wanted to pace development of Fearrington Village so he could stay busy until he was 85. He miscalculated. He's 90 and still busy, still building, still interested.

"Work is progressing on the 52-acre parcel we bought last year and named Granville," the name taken from his dwindling inventory of unused North Carolina county names, Fitch said in a fall 2022 newsletter to residents. Granville, to be built off Millcroft at the southern end of Fearrington, will consist of 41 homes of 2,400 to 2,700 square feet on plots of almost an acre each, "larger homesites than we currently provide," Fitch said.

Work was also progressing on improvements to the wastewater treatment plant. "The renovation will extend its life and ensure our compliance with new watershed rules," Fitch said. "Then we'll file with the state's utilities commission to recoup costs, which at this time we estimate to be $4.2 million."

As of the 2020s, Fitch was building 10–12 houses a year. In 2024 Fitch had 21 lots available, not counting Granville. Annual resales are larger, totaling 58 in 2023, for example.

In July 2023, Fitch sold 248 acres immediately east of Fearrington Village to the Triangle Land Conservancy, a private, non-profit organization dedicated to preserving open space, farms, and clean water sources in the Triangle region. The sale means the land won't be developed—no housing subdivisions, no stores or offices. The land was appraised at $5.449 million, and Fitch sold it to TLC for $3.25 million, said Bo Howes, director of land protection and stewardship (west) for the conservancy. Fitch took a charitable deduction for the remaining value.

## Eleven. The Future

Fitch had bought the land 15 or 20 years earlier and said, "It just seemed like a logical thing for the nature conservancy to have it."

"The long-term plan for that property is undecided right now," Howes said. The conservancy will meet with neighbors to assess their thoughts on the matter. "It could be decided we're not going to do anything with the property. If I were to bet, I would think it would be open to the public with some trails on it within five years or so. Anything we do would be a very light touch on that property."

As for the rest of Fearrington, Fitch said he has enough capacity to keep building for about 15 years. At 90, R.B. doesn't expect to be around for all that time. The burden will fall to Greg, Keebe, and Kelley. After them? "I haven't got that far," he said. In the meantime, R.B. has been preparing for the change, giving Greg more responsibilities. Greg has a background that should help. He has a master's degree in business administration from Northwestern University, but he can be forgiven if he feels like the guys who followed legendary predecessors such as UCLA basketball coach John Wooden or, closer to home, UNC coach Dean Smith.

The Fearrington Homeowners Association has a futures committee that now is looking at two different aspects of the future. The first is what happens after Fitch dies. And the second is "do we have the right governance model" for a still-growing village, said Rose Krasnow, president in 2022–23 of the homeowner's association.

"My concern, going into the future, is how do we keep the very special atmosphere that is Fearrington Village?" Krasnow said. For example, "I think people love turning in and seeing the cows and seeing the silo" as they enter the village. But would anyone, once R.B. Fitch is gone, want to keep that part of the village? The homeowners' association is "wondering if there is any way that we could assume the care and feeding of the animals." While there will be some reduction in the herd to accommodate Granville, the animals will stay, R.B. said.

Residents also express concerns about maintenance of pathways and Jenny's Park. "Its beauty is highlighted in books, promotions, and artworks," a 2020 FHA village attractiveness report noted. But, the report continued, "are there long-term plans for guaranteeing it stays a central park? Will there be adequate funds to maintain its ponds, trails, and gardens?"

Fitch's expansion plans worry many Fearrington residents, who fear increased traffic in the village and strain on amenities such as the village shops, swimming pool, tennis courts, walking trails, and the like. Krasnow drew applause from residents at a community meeting in June 2022 when she said, "We want to make sure growth impacts quality of life favorably" and "It's the amenities in this village that make it so special."

The Covid pandemic that began in 2020 forced a reduction in hours for the village shops and restaurants. For now, the move to operation five days a week in the village, four for the restaurant and inn, seems to be working, and "we're happy with the mix of businesses that we have," said Greg Fitch.

Still R.B. has said that many of the village shops are marginally profitable. So might there be changes in the village? Drastic changes might endanger the draw for weddings and special events, but they also might induce more residents to come to the village.

"Having an informed view of the future plans Fitch Creations has for the Village is essential going forward," the community attractiveness report said, calling for close communication between Fitch Creations and the FHA. "It is in everyone's best interest to keep the Village profitable, vibrant, attractive, and relevant." In return, "we should make a concerted effort to support the businesses within the Village and be mindful of Fitch Creations' many contributions to the Fearrington community."

In the typical subdivision procedure, developers turn over the common land to a homeowners association, though they are not required to do so under North Carolina law. The process may take two or three years. The developer wants to maintain control long enough to make sure the development keeps its appeal to buyers. Also, the HOA needs enough homeowners to sustain the cost of a takeover. But most developers don't want to wait too long to relieve themselves of the expense of maintaining the common areas.

Fitch hasn't been in a hurry about this; he has been turning over land to the Fearrington Homeowners Association gradually for more

## Eleven. The Future

than 30 years, partly because he is still selling houses and wants control. And the FHA has been happy to gradually assume the costs of taking over. "It's a very unusual relationship," Krasnow said. But she expects Fitch will be turning over more land in the next few years, including mail kiosks. "We are in charge of four of them, and we'll end up being in charge of more," Krasnow said. The one on Creekwood needs repair, and one bid came in at $147,000, well above the $50,000 the FHA had estimated. The association regrouped and came up with a new plan in 2023 that it hoped could be accomplished for $90,000. The Gathering Place may need to be expanded as the village adds residents, Krasnow said. When the Weathersfield neighborhood held a holiday party pre-pandemic, they had to limit attendance to keep within the fire code, she said.

Thirty-eight percent of residents surveyed in 2023 said they would like to see a dog park in the village, while 34 percent suggested adding a performance venue.

Neighborhoods are beginning to institute caps on rentals out of concern over investment companies buying properties to rent "because they don't really care about keeping the unit up to snuff," Krasnow said. It's a problem not particular to Fearrington. About two dozen companies have acquired more than 40,000 properties in North Carolina as of early 2022, according to an investigation by the *News & Observer* and the *Charlotte Observer*. One state lawmaker introduced a bill that would cap at 100 the number of single-family homes people or businesses could buy in the state's most populous counties. The measure was opposed by the speaker of the state house and hadn't passed as of mid–2023, but it displayed the concern many people have over the issue.

Krasnow expects that Fearrington will see more younger residents who "will want some different things than what we have here now." While some current residents aren't thrilled about that, Krasnow sees some "real positives" from the energy younger people can provide a community.

But the homes in Granville will start at $750,000, Greg Fitch has said, which will likely draw older, wealthier people than young families and likely not first-time home buyers, who are "vanishing" across

## Fearrington

the country, according to the National Association of Realtors. In 2022, the share of first-time buyers dropped to 26 percent from 40 percent historically, the NAR said.

R.B. Fitch's vision is now about 85 percent complete. Greg said he's now dealing with an established community, and his plan is "steady as she goes." For the inn he wants to continue to offer "an authentic hospitality experience, a sense of getting away."

"I assume given that, as his father is still living, that he will probably try to continue in his father's footsteps," Krasnow said of Greg. "And I think he perhaps appreciates some of the things his mother did and would want to continue them."

As fewer houses are built, revenue will have to depend more on resales, the village events, and patronage of the inn and restaurant, though R.B. said the company might turn to remodeling, which is how he got his start years ago.

Fearrington Village will be a smaller part of a growing county and will grow more slowly than the rest of Chatham County, said Greg Fitch. Climate and lower housing prices are still a draw for many people from the North and West. North Carolina added 133,088 residents in the year ended July 1, 2022, according to U.S. Census Bureau estimates. Only Texas, with 470,708 new residents, and Florida, with 416,754, added more people in that time. (Total U.S. population at the start of 2023 was 334,233,854, the Census Bureau said.) Almost 100,000 more people moved into North Carolina from other states than left it, according to the Census Bureau, reflecting a trend of the last several years.

Most new North Carolina residents are from Florida, New York, Virginia, South Carolina and California, according to census data. Among those five states, residents from South Carolina were most likely to be North Carolina natives, while new residents from New York were the least likely to be North Carolina–born.

While transplants add much to the state's growth, natives are also more likely to stay than in many other states. "Only Texas has a higher share of native-born adults who are still living in the state," Rebecca Tippett, founding director of Carolina Demography at the Carolina Population Center at UNC Chapel Hill told the *News &*

## Eleven. The Future

*Observer* in 2019. "North Carolina is what we consider both a sticky state and a magnet state. So, we're appealing to lots of people for lots of different reasons," Tippett said.

North Carolina remains attractive to retirees, drawing 9.6 percent of retirees who chose to retire outside their state in 2022, second only to Florida with 11.8 percent, according to HireAHelper, a company that provides loading and unloading services for people who are moving.

The Raleigh region is already one of the fastest growing regions in the country and is attracting companies that in turn are attracted by the number of college graduates produced by local universities, all of which gives the Raleigh area "the fourth highest concentration of college graduates of the 50 largest metro areas, trailing only Seattle, San Francisco and Washington, D.C.," the *News & Observer* wrote in November 2021. This emphasis on education in the

Tony Daniels, representing the Fearrington Homeowners Association, presents a large thank-you card to (from left) Greg Fitch, Kelley Fitch, R.B. Fitch, and Laura Morgan from dozens of village residents in May 2024 marking the 50th anniversary of the beginning of the village and thanking them "for all you have done to make Fearrington the wonderful place that we all love." Fitch responded, "It is a real comfort knowing that so many folks enjoy living here, makes 50 years worthwhile" (Fitch Creations).

region is likely to continue. The North Carolina Department of Commerce projects that from 2021 to 2030 occupations requiring a master's, doctoral, or professional degree are likely to grow by 13.6 percent, more than occupations requiring a bachelor's degree, 12.4 percent, an associate degree or credential, 9.8 percent, or a high school diploma or less, 7.4 percent.

Chatham County grew by more than 20 percent from 2010 to 2022 to a population of some 78,000, according to the census. Like the state and the nation, Chatham County is growing more urban, although North Carolina has the second largest rural population of any state, 3,474,661 behind only Texas with 4,744,808.

The Raleigh metropolitan area grew 84.6 percent from 2000 to 2022, according to Axios Raleigh. From 2019 to 2021, the area population grew 2.4 percent, second only to Austin, Texas, 3.0 percent, among the top 15 U.S. metropolitan percentage gainers. But saying North Carolina is growing more urban needs a qualifier: It actually may be growing more suburban. Johnston County in the Raleigh suburbs was the fastest growing county in the state between 2010 and 2020, according to census data. The 2020 pandemic spurred movement to the suburbs nationwide as people were able to work from home and no longer needed to live near their places of work in cities. The office is a "tough sell," wrote *New York Times* columnist Farhad Manjoo. "Remote work seems to be turning from a pandemic necessity into a permanent feature of the American workplace." This situation could make developments like Fearrington more attractive, driving up housing prices.

Former Chatham County planning director Keith Megginson rates Fearrington as suburban, but it has some characteristics of the country life and the urban life. From the quiet of their homes among the trees and hills, most Fearrington residents can walk to a bank, the spa, the bookstore, the Belted Goat, the inn, the Dovecote, the Roost. True, some other perks of the true city life aren't walkable: there is no post office, laundry, grocery store, or drug store within walking distance, but those enterprises are within a short drive of the village. Nearby are major college sports venues at the University of North Carolina, NC State University, and Duke University. The

## Eleven. The Future

North Carolina Symphony holds many of its concerts in Raleigh and Chapel Hill and there is a professional repertory theater, The Playmakers, in Chapel Hill. Such opportunities may well appeal to people who seek the urban-lite life, assuring a steady flow of newcomers.

Chatham County has so many more people than a few years ago that "my small town doesn't feel quite as small as it used to," one long-time Chatham resident told Voices of Chatham, an oral history project. "Sometimes I'm like, 'My God, when will the people stop coming? There's so many of them.'"

Well, they're not going to stop. Continued growth seems assured with Chatham Park in Pittsboro promising to add 60,000 people in the next 25 years and new subdivisions coming to serve the Vinfast electrical vehicle plant to open in 2025 providing 7,500 jobs, and the Wolfspeed plant, which will make silicon carbide wafers providing some 1,800 new jobs by 2030. The North Carolina Office of State Budget and Management projects that Chatham County's population will reach 89,167 by 2030 and 102,379 by 2040. The county will become more densely populated. Already in North Carolina, "no county has enough affordable housing to meet

The Dovecote decorated for Christmas. The Dovecote sells high-end women's clothing. The building also houses the Nest for home goods and Sprout for children's clothing (photograph by Colin Doherty).

the needs of its residents with the lowest incomes," according to the Urban Institute.

"We're going to be in a period of growth," said Anthony Jackson, the Chatham County superintendent of schools. "For some it will be unprecedented. For some it will be exciting. For some it will be a challenge. And for most all of us it will be a period of dynamic shifts."

Just a few miles to the north of Fearrington Village, Chapel Hill is also growing. "Once a small college town, Chapel Hill is transforming into an economic hub in its own right, with new office buildings, co-working spaces, and apartment buildings to rival its neighbors in Durham, and attract investor dollars and new talent," the *News & Observer* wrote in mid–2023.

Climate change may also contribute to growth in the region. If people eschew coastal regions subject to rising ocean levels and places such as Florida that are threatened by hurricanes, they may in turn choose less vulnerable areas, such as central North Carolina. The average cost of homeowners insurance is $4,000 a year in New Orleans and $5,000 in Miami, for example. In North Carolina it was $2,325 per year. The national average was $1,820 per year. "Armed with climate studies, many retirees are looking for communities that are less likely to experience extreme weather events," the *New York Times* reported in late 2022.

Like the nation's population, Chatham County is growing older. The share of people 65 and older in the county rose 37.6 percent from 2011 to 2021, according to Carolina Demography. The mean age of Fearrington residents is 72.6 years according to the 2023 FHA amenities survey.

Fearrington Village has unquestionably contributed to changing Chatham County, making it richer, more educated, more liberal, actually. And that has contributed to making North Carolina more progressive. The state is "halfway between Virginia and the Deep South," H.L. Mencken wrote in 1935. North Carolina has been called the bluest of the red states, a purple state of the "New South." But writers have been writing about a "New South" since Appomattox, and while much has changed, a lot hasn't. What hasn't

## Eleven. The Future

changed, though, appears to be more of an urban-rural divide than a North-South one, and Fearrington is a part of that, the urbanization of the state.

As Fearrington heads into the future, R.B. Fitch isn't looking much into the past. "I've got no rearview mirror," he said. "I know there are things I should have done differently. I know there are things I could have done better, but as I say, I don't look back much. I just sort of move on."

He expressed satisfaction in what he has achieved. "I think we've done a pretty good job. I think we've melded into the fabric of the county very well," he said. "I don't know anybody that's not pleased with sort of where we are and what we've done."

Maybe not everyone, but certainly most.

As Mark Ashness from CE Group summed it up: "The attention to detail clearly shows this was a labor of love for R.B. and his family."

# Appendix: Documents Related to Fearrington Village

Item 1: A retyped county commission minutes when they approved the rezoning for the village in 1974.

Excerpt from Chatham County Board of Commissioners meeting, September 16, 1974.

The following commissioners attended, to wit: Earl. J. Dark, Gordon White, Earl Thompson and Ben Wimberly.

Commissioner Dark recognized approximately 30 citizens from North-East Chatham. Hubert Oakley stated they were present to ask the commissioners to contact Triangle 'J' Planning Dept., and have a study done on the proposed Planned Unit Development to be constructed on the Fearrington Farm. He explained that such a study would take about six months to complete but this would help the people in his community to better understand how the results of such a development would effect the county. Those further urging that the study be made were: Mrs. Jean Hudson, Mrs. Mary Henley, Mrs. Nell Stroud and Mrs. Myra Miska.

Marshall Happer, Attorney for Bell Design Associates spoke stating that his clients had been planning for approximately forty years and they certainly would not do anything on this property that the county would not be proud of later. He further stated that they could not build the first home without proper water and sewage.

After hearing others from the group Commissioner Wimberley stated that he had given the Planned Unit Development a lot of thought and consideration and he would like to make a motion that a resolution be made to approve the application of Bell Smith Design for a Conditional Use Permit on the proposed Planned Unit Development. White seconded the motion. A roll call vote was given with all voting aye except Thompson who abstained from voting. The motion was carried. (copy of the resolution attached.

Hubert Oakley then stated that he was resigning as a member of the Board of Adjustments.

There being no further business the meeting was adjourned at 9:15 P.M. to meet again on October 7, 1974 at 10:00 A.M.

Signed by Earl J. Dark, Sr., Vice Chr.

Chatham County Commissioners

And

Betty West

Clerk to the Board

# Appendix: Documents Related to Fearrington Village

## Item 2: A copy from the county files of the rezoning approval.

BE IT RESOLVED BY THE BOARD OF COMMISSIONERS OF CHATHAM COUNTY, NORTH CAROLINA, AS FOLLOWS:

WHEREAS, an application has been filed for a conditional use permit to establish a planned unit development upon the farm of Jesse O. Fearrington, and the board of commissioners after having first held a public hearing makes the following findings.

1. That Bell-Smith, a partnership of Wake County, North Carolina, holder of an option upon approximately 650 acres of land known as Jesse O. Fearrington Farm applied for a conditional use permit to establish a planned unit development upon said 650 acres of land.

2. That a public hearing was held on July 29, 1974 at 7:30 o'clock p.m. at the courthouse in Pittsboro, North Carolina with the planning board being represented by C. E. Durham.

3. That many people were present, some of whom spoke in favor of and some of whom spoke against the application for the Fearrington farm.

4. That Bell-Smith partnership at the time of filing the application, held an option upon approximately 650 acres of land owned by Jesse O. Fearrington, J. Bunn Fearrington and Edwin M. Fearrington, said land being located on the east side of U. S. Highway 15-501, adjacent to the North Chatham Volunteer Fire Department.

5. That the Fearrington farm was a beautiful property with unique characteristics in historical qualities deserving of preservation. It lies well for residential housing, but its slopes require a builder who is able to cope with them and also

## Appendix: Documents Related to Fearrington Village

an owner who is willing to accept a suitable plan for development. Richard Bell Design Group has done much work in planning a development at said location which would be built around the saving of all the present facilities and most of the trees. His group plans to establish principally single-family detached housing but some singly-family attached housing along with a school site, church site, crafts area and perhaps a convenience store. There will be no motel or shopping center.

    6. That Richard Bell Design Group, the designer of the project has broad experience in planning development and house design. His group has studied the feasibility of developing this property and found that it is a good location for a new community.

    7. Mr. Leister, a member of Richard Bell Design Group did some of the planning for this project and advised that about 125 acres would be left as it is at present so that the appearance from the road would not be materially changed. The resulting density from the plan will call for no more than three units per acre. It will have a community water system and individual septic tanks or such sewage treatment facilities as may be required by the appropriate county and state agencies.

    8. That the property in question is well suited for the establishment of a planned unit development described by applicant because of its size, topography, road network and geographical location.

    9. That the board has studied the report of the County Planner upon this proposed project and has visited a planned unit development in Wake County known as Kildaire Farms.

    10. That the application is in order and meets the requirements of all pertinent directives.

    That the Board, based upon the foregoing findings, does hereby approve the application of Bell-Smith Design Group for a planned unit development for the 650 acres more or less known as the Jesse O. Fearrington farm in Williams Township, Chatham County, North Carolina and do hereby grant the conditional use permit requested in the application.

    The foregoing resolution was introduced by Commissioner *Wimberly*, seconded by Commissioner *White* and duly adopted at a meeting of the Board of Commissioners on September 16, 1974.

# Appendix: Documents Related to Fearrington Village

Item 3: Letter from architect Jon Condoret upon coming to work full-time for R.B. Fitch.

## JON ANDRE CONDORET, A.I.A., C.S.I.
311 N. COLUMBIA ST
CHAPEL HILL, N.C. 27514

June 5, 1981

Fitch Creations, Inc.
203 North Greensboro Street
Carrboro, North Carolina 27510

Dear R.B.:

After having spent most of my professional career as an architect designing houses in the 3000 to 5000 square foot range, I welcomed the opportunity to work with you in designing smaller but more livable houses with good proportionate kitchen space and ample storage. Quite a challenge.

I particularly relished the Fitch Creations' approach of having multiple critiques of the floor plans. This approach led to the elimination of two floor plans that I thought very good at first study.

The new concept that we adopted for Phase IV, that of completely designing each cul de sac first for sun tempering, then for privacy, and then for spacial sculpture is extremely interesting.

I am very concerned that fewer and fewer people can afford housing and can appreciate the fact that you are trying to keep the cost down by creative development.

Thanks for the opportunity to be part of the team.

Sincerely yours,

Jon Condoret

## Appendix: Documents Related to Fearrington Village

Item 4: A typical floor plan for a house in Beechmast, copied from a promotional journal that Fitch Creations produced.

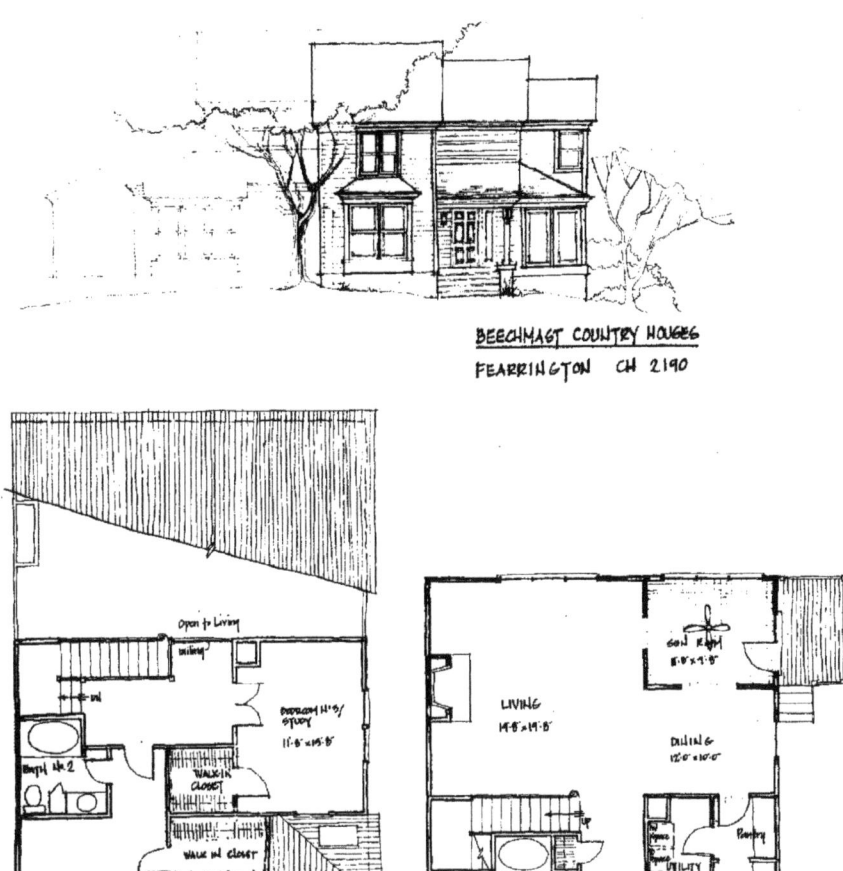

# Appendix: Documents Related to Fearrington Village

Item 5: A page from the Fearrington House Restaurant menu circa 1980. I included it because of the mention of brown bagging, which is discussed in the book.

8) Baked Oysters  $5.15
   with bacon, onion, corn, and tomatoes
9) Pan Fried Trout (or broiled)  $6.15
   fresh from Robbinsville, N.C. - served with rice and a vegetable of the season
10) Spinach Crepe  $4.95
    filled with ham and mushrooms and served with a salad

### Homemade Desserts

Bourbon Pecan Pie, Strawberry Shortcake, and Homemade Ice Cream  $1.25 each

### Beverages

Carbonated Drinks    $.60
Tea, Coffee, Milk    $.60
Orange & V-8 Juice   $.75

- Corkage fee for wine    $2.50 per bottle
- Brown bagging fee       $2.00 per glass & ice

North Carolina law requires patrons to pour their own drinks.

Brown Bagging before 1 P.M. on Sundays prohibited by North Carolina law.

*Appendix: Documents Related to Fearrington Village*

Item 6: A resolution by the Chatham County Commissioners supporting R.B. Fitch's request to have mixed drink sales at the Fearrington House Restaurant.

## COUNTY OF CHATHAM

#95-15

COMMISSIONERS
UVA HOLLAND, Chair
BETTY WILSON, Vice Chair
HENRY DUNLAP
JOHN GRIMES
MARGARET BRYANT POLLARD

BEN SHIVAR
County Manager

ROBERT L. GUNN
County Attorney

Phone (919) 542-8200

P. O. BOX 87
PITTSBORO, N. C. 27312
ORGANIZED 1770    707 SQUARE MILES

### Resolution Supporting A Request for Special Legislation to Provide for the Sale of Mixed Drinks at the Market and Fearrington House Restaurants

**WHEREAS**, Mr. R. B. Fitch over a number of years has planned, designed, and constructed a planned unit development in northern Chatham County known as Fearrington Village containing residential properties and supporting commercial development; and

**WHEREAS**, included in the developed properties are two excellent restaurants, the Market and the Fearrington House, the latter of which is rated a four-star, four-diamond by Triple A and is one of only 50 restaurants to receive this designation in the United States; and

**WHEREAS**, due to the outstanding service and reputation of these restaurants, they serve not only local, but national and international customers; and

**WHEREAS**, to further enhance the service provided by these restaurants, Mr. R. B. Fitch has requested that special legislation in the North Carolina General Assembly be enacted to provide for the sale of mixed beverages at the Market and Fearrington House Restaurants;

**NOW, THEREFORE BE IT RESOLVED** that the Chatham County Board of Commissioners supports the request of Mr. R. B. Fitch for special legislation to permit the sale of mixed beverages at the Market and Fearrington House Restaurants;

**BE IT FURTHER RESOLVED**, that a copy of this resolution shall be forwarded to the Chatham County Legislative delegation to the North Carolina General Assembly.

This the 27th day of March, 1995.

Uva R. Holland, Chair

Betty F. Wilson, Vice Chair

Henry H. Dunlap, Commissioner

John Grimes, Commissioner

Margaret B. Pollard, Commissioner

# Appendix: Documents Related to Fearrington Village

Item 7: A resolution by the Fearrington Homeowners Association stating that the village qualifies under state law to have mixed drink sales.

**The Fearrington Homeowners Association**

November 21, 1995

Mr. Ken Gilliam
Compliance Director
Alcoholic Beverage Control Commission
P O Box 26687
Raleigh, NC 27611

**Special ABC Area**

The Board of Directors of the Fearrington Homeowners Association, Inc., a not-for-profit association of lot owners in the Fearrington Planned Unit Development, Williams Township, Chatham County, North Carolina hereby certify that:

1. The Fearrington Planned Unit Development qualifies as a special ABC area under North Carolina General Statute 18B-101(13a):

   a. It has approximately 1,000 individually owned lots and more than 500 permanent residents. It is an unincorporated area.

   b. It is located in a county where ABC stores have heretofore been established but in which the sale of mixed beverages has not been approved; that borders on a county that has approved the sale of alcoholic beverages countywide and contains an international airport; and borders on Moore County where ABC stores have heretofore been established by petition pursuant to law; and contains 1,063 contiguous acres more or less, an unincorporated area made up of privately owned land and land owned by the association.

   c. The Association is exempt from income tax on its membership income under Article 4 of chapter 105 of the General Statutes, has approximately 1,000 members, was created for municipal and recreational purposes, and has levied assessments or dues since 1978 and has provided the following municipal services: mowing and maintenance of common areas, easements and rights of way; maintaining "The Gathering Place", a building for meetings and functions of the Association since 1990; used its authority under the restrictive covenants to maintain architectural control, animal control among others; and provided limited street lighting.

2. The Board of Directors of the Fearrington Homeowners Association hereby certify that they called and conducted a special meeting of the Association on November 12, 1995, to vote on approving the sale of mixed beverages in the

BOX 26, FEARRINGTON POST, PITTSBORO, NC 27312

*Appendix: Documents Related to Fearrington Village*

3. The Board of directors of the Fearrington Homeowners Association hereby certify that a quorum of over 10 percent of the lot owners was present at the meeting at 2:45 pm. and that a ballot with a map attached of the proposed special ABC area was given to each lot owner attending. (The Board certifies that attachment B is a copy of the ballot.) A large map of the special ABC area was exhibited at the meeting. (The Board certifies that attachment C is the large map exhibited at the meeting.)

4. The Board of Directors of the Fearrington Homeowners Association hereby certify that a majority of Association members present approved the sale of mixed beverages in the Special ABC Area. The vote was 214 to approve the sale and 4 against.

This, the _21_ day of November 1995.

FEARRINGTON HOMEOWNERS ASSOCIATION, INC.

_____
James F. Perry, Vice-president

_____
Kathryn Donahue, secretary

NORTH CAROLINA

_Orange_ COUNTY

I, a Notary Public of the County and State aforesaid, certify that _Kathryn Donahue_ personally came before me this day and acknowledged that she is the Secretary of FEARRINGTON HOMEOWNERS ASSOCIATION, INC., a North Carolina corporation, and that by authority duly given and as the act of the corporation, the foregoing instrument was signed in its name by its President, sealed with its corporate seal and attested by her as its Secretary.

Witness my hand and official stamp or seal, this _21_ day of _November_, 1995.

My Commission Expires: _12-757_      _____
                                     Notary Public

# Appendix: Documents Related to Fearrington Village

Item 8: Notification of a special membership meeting to vote on approval of a "special ABC area."

SPECIAL MEETING OF MEMBERSHIP
FEARRINGTON HOMEOWNERS ASSOCIATION
November 12, 1995, 2:45pm
Fearrington Barn

The special meeting of the members of the Fearrington Homeowners Association has been called by the Board of Directors and notice given in accordance with the by-laws at the request of Fitch Creations, Inc. The purpose of the meeting is for members present to vote on approval of a "Special ABC area" as defined in G.S. 18B-603 (f2). Such approval will allow Fitch Creations, Inc. to apply for issuance of a mixed-drink permit by the North Carolina Alcoholic Beverage Control Commission for the sale of mixed beverages at the restaurants within Fearrington Planned Unit Development.

The area considered the Special ABC Area is shown on the attached map and is described as follows:

All that area east of the eastern right-of-way of US 15-501, Williams Township, Chatham County, North Carolina shown as the Fearrington farm in 1975 when conveyed to Fitch Creations, Inc., plus all adjacent land conveyed to Fitch Creations, Inc., from that year to date and in total now known as Fearrington Planned Unit Development. This includes Fearrington Village Center, Fearrington Section I through Section VIII, Fearrington Woods and land still owned by Fitch Creations, Inc., but yet to be developed.

Specifically excluded from this Special Area are adjoining tracts of land which have neither been conveyed to Fitch Creations, Inc., nor are now a part of the Fearrington Planned Unit Development (shown as "out parcel.").

---

BALLOT

TO PERMIT THE SALE OF MIXED BEVERAGES IN THE SPECIAL ABC AREA SHOWN AS FEARRINGTON PLANNED UNIT DEVELOPMENT ON THE MAP IN WILLIAMS TOWNSHIP, CHATHAM COUNTY, NORTH CAROLINA.

___ FOR
___ AGAINST

## Appendix: Documents Related to Fearrington Village

Item 9: A map of a major walking trail in Fearrington Village.

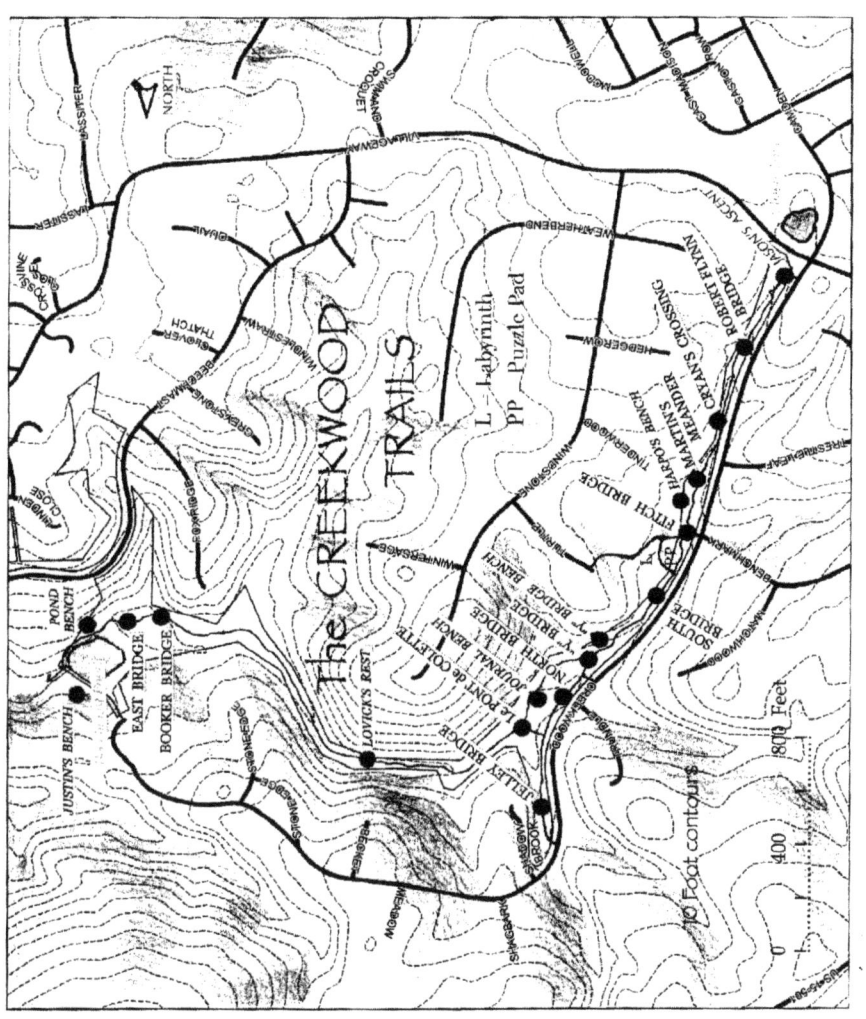

Appendix: Documents Related to Fearrington Village

Item 10: An award to the Fitches from the Fearrington Homeowners Association.

# Author's Note on Sources

My aim is to appeal to a general reader and not impede the writing with footnotes or repetitive attributions. Therefore, I decided to have this separate section on the sourcing. The key to my research has been interviews with most of the people quoted, mostly in person but sometimes by phone and/or email. In these interviews, people were mostly relying on memory, which can be faulty, though I have tried to check matters with more than one source and with documents. What I've produced, I believe, is as authentic as you can get it.

The main sources are the in-person interviews I did in 2021–23 with R.B. Fitch, Keebe Fitch, and Greg Fitch, Laura Morgan, Dan Sears, Theresa Chiettini, Jess Fearrington, Jill and Bill Wargin, and Rose Krasnow, and I also exchanged emails and phone calls with them. I also interviewed in person Eric Andrews, Michael Cotter, Nathalie Dupree, Ginny Gregory, Anne Fitch Havens, Kirstine Lindemann, George Malacinski, Keith Megginson, Paul Messick, Karen Metzguer, Paula de Pano, Ed Price, Bob Strowd, and Doug Zabor. I interviewed Anne Anger, Evy Barrow, Gerald Bell, Phillip Cheeseman, Michael Crowell, Chris Culbreth, Sally Earnest, William Fischel, Clyde Frazier, Luther Hodges, Robert Holton, Karen Howard, Bo Howes, Jaye Kreller, Howard Lee, Jane Marlow, Ruth Moose, Marva Price, Jeanne Riddle, Deepa Sanyal, Arielle Schecter, Emily Silverman, George Smart, Mandy Summerson, Gloria Wilkins, Regina Yeager, and Bob Zimmer by phone, email or both. I exchanged emails with Mark Ashness, Ben Barker, and Moreton Neal.

I recorded many of these interviews. R.B. declined to be recorded. "I might say something stupid," he said. After a few of our conversations I noted that he hadn't said anything stupid. "Just give me time," he said. He never did say anything stupid.

# Author's Note on Sources

R.B. did allow Elizabeth Millwood of the Southern Oral History Program at UNC to record him for three interviews in 2011, and I quote from them extensively. Whoever persuaded Fitch to do the interviews provided a valuable service to the history of this region and the state.

I went through the files on Fearrington at the Chatham County Planning Department and checked minutes of county commissioners' meetings. They are available going back to 1868 at https://www.chathamcountync.gov/government/board-of-commissioners/-commissioner-meetings/board-minutes-by-year.

The Chatham County library in Pittsboro has files of newspaper articles on various aspects of county life, including a notebook on Fearrington. The articles are from a variety of newspapers, and sometimes they are not specified as to which newspaper or are not dated. Also, the collection is not definitive, as there could be relevant articles not included, but still it was helpful. The library is a wonderful resource for the county and a most comfortable place to work and browse, and the librarians are knowledgeable and happy to help. I also checked back issues of the *Chatham News* and *Chatham Record* at the *Chatham News + Record* office in Siler City.

I consulted the files at the Fearrington Homeowners Association, particularly association newsletters, which is where I found a promotional video on Fearrington done in the early 1990s. Carl Stromee, an original Fearrington resident, prepared a couple of papers on the history of Fearrington with information from Jesse Fearrington. A version of his work, augmented with information from Jesse Fearrington, Jr., and Fitch Creations, appears on the Fearrington Homeowners Association website, https://fearringtonfha.org/history-of-fearrington-village/.

I also watched a memorial video about Jon Condoret produced by his daughter, Arielle Condoret Schechter, at https://vimeo.com/319567406.

A Google search on zoning history produced numerous authoritative articles, including summaries of *Euclid v. Amber Realty*.

Through Google I also found relevant articles in *Gourmet* magazine, *Our State* magazine, and *Chatham* magazine.

*Author's Note on Sources*

I also consulted the websites for Fearrington Village, Fearrington.com, and Fearrington Cares, FearringtonCares.org.

I consulted the Chatham County Historical Association website where there is a video on the history of the Fearrington Farm presented by Galloway Ridge resident Bill Sharpe: https://chathamhistory.org/resources/Documents/PDFs/ResearchArticles/HistoryofFearringtonFarm.pdf. The historical association has a wealth of information about Chatham County history online.

Much information about the animals in the village comes from an article in the November 2022 *Belted Gazette*, the FHA newsletter, by Jenny Walker.

Footnote to the liquor-by-the-drink issue: Many North Carolina lawmakers had for years considered support for liquor-by-the-drink the kiss of death for their political careers. But after the legislature passed the local option measure in 1978, by early 1979 mixed drink sales were approved by voters in several counties, including Mecklenburg, Orange, Wake, Durham, and New Hanover, and in many cities, including Asheville, Calabash, Greensboro, High Point, Sanford, Southern Pines, and Sunset Beach. Mixed drink elections failed at that time only in Dare and Alamance counties and in the cities of Black Mountain, Burlington and Graham. Michael Crowell, "A History of Liquor-By-The-Drink Legislation in North Carolina," *Campbell Law Review* 1 (1979).

# Chapter Notes

## Preface

Percentage of U.S. population in the South from *A New History of the American South*, p 493.

Coclanis quote from *"A New History*, p. 495.

## Chapter One

R.B. Fitch comments are from my interviews and the oral history project.

The farm in the 19th century from the Stromee papers.

On dairy farming from Jesse Fearrington, Jr.

On the Fitch land purchase, Chatham County deed book 386, page 112, and email from Paul Messick, Oct. 7, 2022.

Information and commissioners' comments and votes on Bell-Smith option, the Planned Unit Development, rezoning request from board of commissioners' minutes of July 29, 1974, Aug. 5, 1974, Aug. 19, 1974, Sept. 16, 1974, May 19, 1975, June 30, 1976, and Sept. 20, 1976, also a resolution of Sept. 16, 1974. Also, *Pittsboro Herald*, July 24, 1974.

Information on the placement of the university and farmers' fear of the railroad comes from a 1970 county land development study and "A History of Chatham County, North Carolina," By Walter D. Siler, available on the Chatham County Historical Association website. https://chathamhistory.org/resources/Documents/PDFs/ResearchArticles/WalterDSilerHistoryofChathambyBrooks.pdf

Population figures from N.C. Digital Collection. https://digital.ncdcr.gov/digital/collection/p15012coll4/id/772

Chatham as a poor county from Chatham County Planning Department document, undated, but probably mid–70s.

Michael Surface from Surface letter of April 21, 1978, in county Planning Department files.

Information on early zoning from June 19, 2012, article by Amanda Erickson, Bloomberg City Lab.

*Village of Euclid v. Amber Realty Co.* from *Encyclopedia of Cleveland History*, Case Western Reserve University. https://case.edu/ech/articles/v/village-euclid-v-ambler-realty-co

Supreme Court comments from https://www.law.cornell.edu/supremecourt/text/272/365

Robert Simon comment from A Brief History of Reston, Virginia, Gulf Reston, Inc. https://mars.gmu.edu/server/api/core/bitstreams/1ba3aee9-bbf5-4f31-892b-0db74ef73e16/content

Mixed use developments are more common now across the country, while often mixing residential with chain stores. Southern Village and Meadowmont in Orange County, North Carolina, are versions of mixed-use communities. Then there are affinity communities such as Serenbe outside Atlanta, which describes itself as a "biophile" community. *Bloomberg Businessweek* (April 20, 2020) described it as "one of a few dozen relatively new utopian-lite communities in the U.S., all echoing a rich tradition that stretches to the American Shaker movement of the 1780s." Such developments have spread around the world in recent years, to about 1,200 in 2016, according to the Foundation for Intentional Community, a nonprofit that provides information and support to

# Chapter Notes

many of these experimental towns, the magazine said. Cynthia Tina, the organization's communications director, told the magazine that "there are currently 753 intentional communities in the U.S. listed in our directory," and the number is probably higher. Examples are Powder Mountain in Utah, aimed at skiers and outdoor lovers and Salmon Creek Farm in Mendocino County, Calif., a 1970s commune being restyled as an arts colony.

Marie Burick comment from June 23, 2016 article, "Building a 'Sense of Community': Why mixed-use developments are sprouting up across the US," by Kim Slowey in *Construction Dive Magazine*. https://www.constructiondive.com/news/building-a-sense-of-community-why-mixed-use-developments-are-sprouting-u/421386/

Fischel comment from my interview.

Robert Dumaine comment from letter of Aug. 5, 1974, to Chatham Planning director Tim Scott.

June Wrenn, "I'm concerned" comment... The *Pittsboro Herald* Aug. 21, 1974. June Wrenn, by the way, was male.

Fitch comment "But the farm is so beautiful," *The Pittsboro Herald* Aug. 21, 1974.

Oakley comment, "This decision..." probably *Pittsboro Herald*, Sept. 18, 1974.

The Herald article says that Commissioner Earl Thompson voted and that a woman complained that he should have abstained because he did construction work for Fitch. The article says Thompson replied that he was willing to abstain but insisted he had no promise of work on the PUD from Fitch and had not asked for any. Seeing no way to resolve this, I chose to go with the minutes.

## Chapter Two

My interviews with R.B. Fitch, Chiettini, Keebe Fitch, Gregory, Wargin, Hodges, Bell, Greg Fitch, Culbreth, Zabor, Cheeseman, de Pano, Morgan, Sears, Mears, Megginson, and R.B. Fitch's comments in the oral history project.

"Better just keep on" Amanda Hoyle, *Triangle Business Journal*, Sept. 20, 2013.

Number of F-100s produced from National Museum of the U.S. Air Force fact sheet.

F-100 accidents. http://www.afsc.af.mil/shared/media/document/AFD-090922-090.pdf

R.B. and Jenny's undergraduate activities from their class yearbooks at UNC.

Fitch Creations structure from corporate filing with N.C. Secretary of State's Office.

Toll comment from obituary, *The Washington Post*, Oct. 11. 2022, by Brian Murphy. https://www.washingtonpost.com/obituaries/2022/10/11/robert-toll-homes-builder-dies/.

For state campaign contributions see https://www.ncsbe.gov/campaign-finance/search-campaign-funding-and-spending-reports-and-penalties.

Federal Elections Commission website for individual federal campaign contributions. https://www.fec.gov/introduction-campaign-finance/-how-to-research-public-records/-individual-contributions/

## Chapter Three

My interviews with Morgan, Bell, R.B. Fitch, Keebe Fitch, Sears, Neal, Callaway, Gregory, Schecter, Smart, Kreller, and the oral history program.

"Houses must feel good..." from Fitch Creations newsletter October 1987.

Richard Bell information from N.C. State School of Design https://design.ncsu.edu/architecture/2020/03/20/in-memoriam-landscape-architect-dick-bell/

Sears bio from Sears and *Spectator Magazine*, November 1989, pp. 29-30.

Jon Condoret background and accent from *Durham Magazine* April 2013, pp. 63-66.

Arthur Larson house, *Durham Magazine*, April 2013.

"Never a cross word..." *Durham Magazine* 2013.

Appearance commission award from Sears Design Group website. https://searsdesigngroup.com/awards.php

Flynn "intuitive common sense" from

## Chapter Notes

Flynn obituary, Mebane Enterprise, Dec. 6, 2012.

"Everyone thinks they're alive..." *Chapel Hill News*, Aug. 17, 1994.

## Chapter Four

Information on the first houses from a Fitch Creations document celebrating their 25th anniversary. One history of Fearrington says the first house ready for viewing was 11 Benchmark. R.B. doesn't remember it that way, and the 2001 document is an invitation to an open house for 12, 13, and 14 Matchwood, in cooperation with their then owners, saying, "The first three model homes in Phase I of the Historic District opened in November 1976. Drop in and visit all three houses."

Other information from oral history program transcript, my interviews with R.B. Fitch, Doug Zabor, Mark Ashness, Gerald Bell, Michael Cotter, Jill Wargin, Bill Wargin, Laura Morgan, Rose Krasnow, Keith Megginson, Eric Andrews, and from *A Country Journal*.

Panelization from *Professional Builder*, November 1976.

"Half of the energy use..." *The Daily Tarheel* Nov. 22, 1977.

Won design award four consecutive years. *Southern Living* Oct. 1979.

The cost of his energy contest from *The Professional Builder*, March 1976.

Kiosks: The result of the kiosks is that most Fearrington residents have two addresses—a Fearrington Post address for the kiosks and a street address. The U.S. Postal Service delivers to the mailboxes in the kiosks, while UPS, FedEx, and Amazon often deliver to the street address, so it helps to know who your shipper will be. The situation is well known to stores in the area. When my wife asked a saleswoman who would be shipping an item we bought, the woman immediately said, "You must be from Fearrington."

## Chapter Five

Much attribution here is in the text. I interviewed in person or by phone Kirstine Lindemann, George Malacinski, Anne Angers, Deepa Sanyal, R.B. Fitch, Bill Wargin, and Laura Morgan.

Data on Chatham longevity from Andrew Van Dam, *The Washington Post*, Sept. 21, 2018, https://www.washingtonpost.com/business/2018/09/21/two-places-maryland-where-people-can-expect-live-longer-average-than-almost-anywhere-else-us/ and from the University of Wisconsin Population Health Institute. Also, "The Effects of Education on Mortality: Evidence Using College Expansions." Jason Fletcher and Hamid Noghanibehambari NBER Working Paper No. 29423 October 2021. https://www.nber.org/system/files/working_papers/w29423/w29423.pdf.

Data on *New Yorker* demographics pulled from the magazine's media kit and from Mediamax in mid–2024.

Voter registration numbers are from the Chatham County Elections Board web site as of April 2024. Election results are also from that web site, https://www.chathamcountync.gov/government/-departments-programs-a-h/elections/-election-results, though for results before 2001 you must consult the hard copy in the files. Also, the state elections board, https://www.ncsbe.gov/

Bitzer comment from a July 19, 2022, article by *New York Times* columnist Frank Bruni.

Demographic data on Fearrington comes from the Census Bureau. The village is a Census Designated Place where the Census Bureau drills down into communities that are smaller than cities or counties: https://www.census.gov/acs/www/data/data-tables-and-tools/data-profiles/. Once there, click on place, then North Carolina, then Fearrington Village from the list of Census Designated Places and pick from the four categories of data that show up. Slide to the right to get the data on Fearrington Village. If you go there and find the numbers are slightly different than mine it's because the Census Bureau is constantly refining its data.

Data on healthy counties comes from the University of Wisconsin County Health Rankings 2023. The data show that counties in the top 10 percent for

# Chapter Notes

Health Outcomes "have more available and better-resourced civic infrastructure, including access to information via broadband internet, libraries and local newspapers, and access to civic spaces, including adequately funded schools, parks and social associations.... For instance, the average county among the healthiest 10 percent has almost twice as much access to parks and recreation facilities, and 24 percent more household access to broadband internet than the least healthy counties. The vast majority of healthier counties (88 percent) have adequate school funding to support student achievement of national average test scores and schools nearly have $9,000 more per student, annually, on average. Healthier counties also have higher rates of voter turnout (more than 30 percent higher) and census participation (more then 40 percent higher) than among the least healthy counties."

## Chapter Six

Quotes are from my interviews with R.B. Fitch, Dan Sears, Chris Culbreth, and Eric Andrews, unless otherwise noted.

"Most residents say it is the attractiveness of the village..." from a 2020 Fearrington Homeowners Association Community Assessment Survey.

"Our plans are..." from article in unidentifiable newspaper. Undated but probably 1984–85.

"There was never an idea about a showplace..." my interview with Sears.

"Sometimes you can't tell..." *Spectator Magazine* Nov. 16, 1989

"The more you can crowd together..." *Spectator Magazine* Nov. 16, 1989.

Designed for "sun-tempering..." Condoret letter to Fitch Creations, June 5, 1981.

"It's about like naming a child..." *The Daily Tarheel*, March 13, 1980.

Added features in Beechmast homes, Fitch Creations promotional documents.

The Woods. Fitch Creations promotional documents.

Savannah "has best land plan..." *Spectator Magazine*, Nov. 16, 1989.

Bush Creek from history of FV by Sears Design Group.

Information on Galloway Ridge beginnings from video produced in 2015 on its 10th anniversary, https://www.youtube.com/watch?v=8Nfb1fkG_co. Also, Aug. 1991 article in unidentified newspaper, probably *Chatham Herald or Record.*

Grace Penny letter to R.B. Fitch from Chatham County Planning Department files.

Information on The Gathering Place, the Fearrington Homeowners Association from FHA notices to residents, "A History of Fearrington Village" by Carl Stromee and Jesse Fearrington, Jr., and a timetable prepared by the FHA on 25th anniversary of the FHA formation.

Opposition to Briar Chapel development from FHA timetable.

Karen Howard comment from *Chatham News+ Record*, Oct. 19, 2022.

Information on Fearrington Cares from its website, interview with Karen Metzguer and Mandy Summerson.

## Chapter Seven

Sources, unless otherwise mentioned, are my interviews or emails with R.B. Fitch, Theresa Chiettini, Laura Morgan, the oral history transcript, Dannye Romine Powell, Moreton Neal, Ginny Gregory, and Ben Barker.

McIntyre's among 15 most beautiful places: The 15 Most Beautiful Places In North Carolina (southernliving.com)

Offered to sell land to the county ... *The Chatham County Herald*, Nov. 11, 1981.

"Get involved in a bigger neighborhood..." *Chapel Hill News*, May 21, 1995.

"I don't think I would be in the restaurant business..." *Flavors of Fearrington*, p. 21.

"Our goal ..." from "A History of Fearrington Village" by Carl Stromee with help from Jesse Fearrington, Jr. March 2011, The Fitches reopened the house in May of 1980.... Jenny Fitch, *The Fearrington House Cookbook* p. xi.

"Most influential Southern Black chef..." Imani Perry, *South to America*,

## Chapter Notes

p. 267. There is now an Edna Lewis Foundation in Savannah, Georgia, which offers scholarships to "extend the legacy of Edna Lewis by creating opportunities for African Americans in the fields of cooking, agriculture, food studies and storytelling."

"Light as a dandelion seed..." Evan Jones, *Gourmet Magazine*, April 1984.

"There weren't many young, educated African-Americans, male or female, deciding to be a chef..." Drew Jackson, *News & Observer*, Feb. 27, 2020.

A succession of talented chefs... Katie Kane, *Our State* magazine, Dec, 2022.

The inn opened in 1986... Jenny Fitch, *The Fearrington House Cookbook*, p. xi.

Criteria for Relais & Chateaux from https://tourismology.blogspot.com/2005/08/relais-chteaux-quaility-standards.html

"Cows were easier..." *Chatham News+Record*, April 13, 2006, plus interview with R.B. Fitch.

"I was looking through National Geographics..." Galloway Ridge video. https://www.youtube.com/watch?v=8Nfb1fkG_co.

Additional information on the animals from article by Fearrington resident Jenny Walker in the FHA newsletter, *The Belted Goat*, November 2022. Also an interview with Bob Strowd.

Information on birds from *Thinking About Fearrington*, pp 10–13.

Information on the trails and pathways from my walking the trails, talking with Colette File, an FHA trail map, and from *Thinking About Fearrington*.

## Chapter Eight

Sources include my interviews with Chip Callaway and Ginny Gregory.

How he would like to be remembered. R.B. Fitch letter to residents, Dec. 16, 1995.

"Can we have a garden wedding..." *Our State* Magazine, April 28, 2011.

"You can do this for a living..." Maria Johnson, *Our State* Magazine, June 2010.

## Chapter Nine

When I asked R.B. Fitch how he got liquor-by-the-drink for the Fearrington House Restaurant well before Chatham County approved such sales, he was vague, said he couldn't remember details, but it had something to do with being in a county next to a county with an international airport, because lawmakers didn't want travelers to think North Carolinians were a bunch of rubes.

As I asked around, one name kept coming up—Howard Lee. First, I found Michael Crowell, who explained how it was done, and he is the source for much of the chapter, plus the legislature's Session Laws of 1995. Then I finally tracked Lee down, who said he couldn't remember specifics either, but essentially confirmed what I had found out.

Information on 1974 and 1980 votes from *News & Observer*, Nov. 2, 1980, and *Chapel Hill Newspaper*, Nov. 5, 1980.

1984 vote totals from Abstract of Votes, Chatham County Board of Elections.

Explanation of the meaning of votes from articles by Cassie H. Wasko, *Chatham Record*, May 10, 1984, and May 17, 1984.

Date of Fearrington wine and beer permit from state ABC Commission.

State legislature approval of local option votes in 1978 from personal knowledge. I covered the issue for *The Charlotte Observer*.

Statewide prohibition 1909. A History of Liquor-by-the-Drink Legislation in North Carolina. Michael Crowell, *Campbell Law Review* 1979.

Support for LBD legislation from county commissioners in resolution of March 27, 1995.

Nov. 12, 1995, vote from FHA letter to state Alcoholic Beverage Control Commission, Nov. 21, 1995.

Permit issued Dec. 12, 1995, from ABC Commission document,

2009 county vote from Chatham Board of Elections website.

# Chapter Notes

## Chapter Ten

My interviews with Jill and Bill Wargin, John Hammond.

Debate about kiosks from "Historical Review of Fearrington," by Carl Stromee, presented to the fifth annual meeting of the Fearrington Homeowners Association, Nov. 10, 1985.

KKK sign—"What's the history of Ku Klux Klan billboards near Smithfield?" by Brooke Cain, *The News & Observer*, April 13, 2022. https://www.newsobserver.com/news/local/article232986152.html

Bruni comment from *New York Times* column of July 24, 2022.

Confederate statue debate from my personal coverage of Chatham County commissioner meetings on the subject.

Details on incorporation debate and Moriarty comment from *Daily Tarheel* Nov. 6, 1990. Cassie H. Wasko, *Chatham Record*, Nov. 6, 1990. *Chatham Record*, unspecified date in 1990, presumably October or November.

Levy a tax of five cents per $100. FAQ document on incorporation, probably prepared by FHA, Dec. 3, 2005.

Final incorporation vote, Fearrington Homeowners Association minutes, Nov. 13, 2005.

Wastewater Treatment plant—My interview with R.B. Fitch.

The Granary. Interviews with R.B. and Keebe Fitch, various Fearrington residents.

Highway bypass information from Chatham County Commissioners' minutes, May 25, 1989.

"Just when you think you can relax…" John Welter, *Chapel Hill Newspaper*, May 10, 1989.

Will Heiser letter to Chatham County manager May 9, 1989.

Petition with 739 signatures—Minutes of Chatham County Board of Commissioners, May 25, 1989.

*Chapel Hill News*, May 26, 1989

Hurricane Fran statistics from WRAL News. https://www.wral.com/-hurricane-fran/17834050/ and National Weather Service. https://www.wral.com/-hurricane-fran/17834050/ Interviews or emails with Jeanne Riddle, Marva Price, Ruth Moose, Laura Morgan, R.B. Fitch, Evy Barrow.

## Chapter Eleven

Annual resales email from Fitch Creations and notes from FHA meeting, Nov. 20, 2022.

Corporate landlords … *News & Observer* Feb. 23, 2023.

North Carolina added 133,088 residents… from Richard Stradling, *News & Observer*, Jan. 3, 2023.

Perspective: North Carolina's Robust, but Uneven, Growth. Ferrell Guillory. March 17, 2023. ednc.org

Second largest rural population… Rebecca Tippett, Carolina Demography, March 21, 2016.

Vinfast and Wolfspeed. *Chatham Magazine*, 2022–23 issue, pp 16–19.

Population growth projections. Population Growth 2030-2040 | NC OSBM

"We're going to be in a period of growth…" *Chatham Magazine* 2022–23, p. 18.

Average cost of homeowners insurance from column by Benjamin Keys, *The New York Times*, May 7, 2023, and from NerdWallet, March 23, 2023.

H.L. Mencken quote from *South to America* by Imani Perry, p. 119.

# Bibliography

## Books

The Book of Fearrington, 2016, by Warren Reed. Good information on the demographics of the area but also information on the birds, flowers, and climate of the region.

Chatham Roots, 2022, Warren Reed. Self-published.

Fearrington. A Country Journal. This book, loose-leaf in its original form, was prepared by Fitch Creations as a promotion and as an introduction to Fearrington for new homeowners.

The Fearrington House Cookbook—A Celebration of Food, Flowers and Herbs, 1987, Jenny Fitch. Dell. A cookbook with many favorite recipes from the Fearrington House but also a page on the history of the village by the woman who helped found it. It is available at McIntyre's, the Belted Goat, and Dovecote.

Flavors of Fearrington, 2004, Fearrington Cares. Also a cookbook but it contains several pages on the history and ambiance of the village.

Lessons from North Carolina, Gene Nichol, 2023. Blair.

A New History of the American South, 2023, W. Fitzhugh Brundage, editor. University of North Carolina Press.

South to America, 2022, Imani Perry. Ecco.

Thinking About Fearrington, n.d., Henry Castner and Frank McKeever. Self-published. This little book is especially good on the flora and fauna of Fearrington, with numerous color photographs.

## Magazines

Campbell Law Review
Chatham Magazine
Construction Dive Magazine
Durham Magazine
Gourmet
Our State
Southern Living
Spectator Magazine

## Newspapers

Chapel Hill News
The Chatham County Herald
Chatham News + Record
Chatham Record
The Daily Tarheel
Mebane Enterprise
The New York Times
The News & Observer
The Pittsboro Herald
Professional Builder
Triangle Business Journal
The Washington Post

## Videos

Arielle Condoret Schecter (October 2010) Jon Condoret Memorial Video (Video) Vimeo https://vimeo.com/319567406

Fitch Creations (circa 1994) Fearrington: A Country Village (video) promotional video on CD in files of Fearrington Homeowners Association

# Bibliography

Galloway Ridge, Bob Zimmer (2015) *Galloway Ridge at Fearrington* (Video) YouTube https://www.youtube.com/watch?v=8Nfb1fkG_co

Galloway Ridge (Undated) *History of Fearrington Farm*, (Video) on Chatham County Historical Association website. https://drive.google.com/file/d/1kwC8PhHqQ7e-KpWVciCurLMBpHkwZZWy/view

The Learning Channel (1992) *Great Country Inns* episode. Fearrington Village (Video) This episode is on the same CD as the Fitch Creations video

Terminus Films (2019) *The Well-Placed Weed: The Bountiful Life of Ryan Gainey* (Video) Vimeo.com/310385881

# Index

Numbers in ***bold italics*** indicate pages with illustrations

Alexander, Kwame  101
Alexander, Rosemary  130
Ambler Realty Co.  22
Andrews, Eric  61, 65, 80
Angers, Anne  69
Arthur Carlsen Charitable Fund  92
Ashness, Mark  19, 60, 159

Barber, Wade  87
Barker, Ben  111–112, 137
Barker, Karen  111–112
Barrow, Evy  61, 146–147
Bedford, Colin  112
Bell, Gerald  34, 37, 40, 42, 45–46, 60
Bell, Richard  16, 22, 25, 42, 46, 76
Bell Design Group  16, 18, 24–26, 46; see also Bell, Richard
Belted Goat  99–100, 137, 156
*Better Homes and Gardens*  8, 47, ***66***
*Bloomberg BusinessWeek*  72
Briar Chapel  10, 20, 91, 142, 144–145
brown-bagging  136, 166
Bruni, Frank  142
Burick, Marie-Claire  24
Burr, Richard  35
Bush, George W.  74
Bush Creek neighborhood  5, 9, 87, 89

Café Nicholson  109–110
Callaway, Chip  44, 126, 128–130, 133–134
Camden (Jenny's) Park  10, 52–***53***, ***77***, 83, 126, 129, ***133***, 151
Camden Park houses  5, 9, 10, 51, ***62***, ***77***, 79, 83, ***84–86***, 87, 91, 126, ***133***
Carolina Population Center  154, 158
Carter, Jimmy  100
Castner, Henry  120, 122
Chapel Hill  3, 4, 8, 10–11, 18–20 24, 27, 36–37, 45, 48, 50, 55, 64–66, 69, 73, 88, 93, 98, 101, 107, 116, 130, 136, 143, 145–146, 148, 157–158
*Chapel Hill News*  18
Chapin, Hugh  88–89
*Charlotte Observer*  101, 153

Chatham County  1, 3–4, 7, 9, 11–12, 15, 17, 19–21, 22, 24–26, 32, 52, 57, 58, 64–66, 71–75, 81–82, 87–89, 91–92, 107, 136, 138–140, 142, 146–147, 154, 156–158
Chatham County Board of Commissioners  25–26, 139
Chatham County Planning Board  24–25
*Chatham Magazine*  112
Chatham Park  19, 157
Cheeseman, Phillip  36–38
chickens  117, ***118***
Chiettini, Theresa  4, 27, 39, 65, 96, 104, 106
Coclanis, Peter A.  3
Cole, Adelaide  7
Cole, Elijah  15,
Cole, William, Jr.  7
Cole, William, Sr.  15
concrete sheep  52, ***53***
Condoret, Joany  47–48
Condoret, Jon  3, 8, 39, 42, ***43***, ***47***, 48–52, ***50–51***, 52, 53, 58, 66, 80–81, 83, ***90***, 93, 100
Continuing Care Residential Community (CCRC)  87
Cotter, Joanne  61
Cotter, Michael  61
Countryhouse Closes  5, 9, 79
Covid  34–36, 39, 94, 102, 104, 152
Creekwood Trail  ***120–121***, ***123***
crime  11–12
Crowell, Michael  137
cul de sacs  80–81
Culbreth, Chris  35, 79

Daniels, Neville (Tony)  ***155***
dairy farming  15–16
Dean & DeLuca  109
DeMaine, Robert  24
De Pano, Paula  36
Dirr, Michael  130
Dole, Elizabeth  35
Dole, Robert  35
Dovecote  143, 156–***157***

**185**

# Index

Duke Center for Living  2, 10, 88
Duke University  11, 47–48, 73, 156
Dupree, Nathalie  111
Durham  3, 10–11, 20, 24, 33, 47–48, 55, 69, 73–74, 88, 112, 115–116, 145–146, 148, 158
Durham County  57
*Durham Magazine*  48, 53

Earnest, Sally  147
Elmers, Renee  35
Euclid, Ohio  22
Eureka Farms  7, 15

F-100  *28*, 29
*Family Circle*  8, 66
farmers' market  13–*14*
Fearrington, Edward M.  15
Fearrington, E.M.  7
Fearrington, Jesse, Jr.  15–16
Fearrington, Jesse, Sr.  4, 7, 15, *16*, 76
Fearrington, John (Bun)  7
Fearrington, John Andrew  15,
Fearrington Pluton  125
Fearrington, Willa  7
Fearrington Cares  10, 13, 90–94, *92*
Fearrington Homeowners Association  8, 9–10, 14, 79, 87, 89–91, 93, 123–124, 139, 151–152
Fearrington House Cookbook  127
Fearrington House Inn  9, 11–12, *13*, 39, 43, 52, 89, 98–99,103–104, 106, 112, *113–115*, 126–127, *132*, 135, 137, 139, 152, 154, 156
Fearrington House Restaurant  8–9, 11, 13, 32, 36, 39, 43, 45, 98–99, 103–104, 106, *107–109*, 112–113, 117, 126, 127, 130, *131*, 134, 136, 137, 139–140, 143, 152
55th Fighter Bomber Squadron  29
File, Colette  120–121
Fischel, William  24
Fitch, Greg  4, 32, 34–35, 39, 41, 53, 119, 127, 151–*155*
Fitch, Jenny  1–3, 8–10, 14, 17, 30–32, *31*, 35–36, 42, *43–44*, 45, 52, *53*, 66, 77, 80, 82, 98, 100, 116, 136; and gardens 126–135, *128*; and restaurant 106–111, *110*, 113
Fitch, Katherine McIntyre  27, 100
Fitch. Keebe  4, 31–32, 37, 42, 44–45, 52, 65, 100–102, 127, 143, 151,
Fitch, Kelley  4, 32, 151, *155*
Fitch, R.B., Jr.  1, 3, 4, 8, 13, 17, 20, 24–26, *33*, 34–35, 42, *43*, 45, 47–49, 51–53, 55, 57, 62, 64–65, 68, 70–71, 75–77, 80–83, *81*, 86–90, 96, 98–99, 102–103, 106–107, 109, 111, 117, 126, 141, 143, 145–146, 148–152, *155*, 159; as Air Force pilot *28–30*; birth 27; as a boss 36–40;

buys Fearrington farm 18; energy saving efforts 58–60, *66–67*; gets mixed drinks 136–140; marriage 32; opens inn 112–115, *113–115*; opens restaurant 106–109
Fitch, R.B., Sr.  27
Fitch Creations  7–10, 27, 32, 37–*38*, 47, 57, 63–65, 82, 87, 96, 104, 106, 123, 134, 145, 152
Fitch Energy Monitor  58, *59*
Fitch Lumber Co.  27, 57
*Flavors of Fearrington*  94, 132
Florida  29, 154–155, 158
Flynn, Robert  3, 9, 34, 39, 53–*54*, 131, 135
*Forbes Travel Guide*  113
*Foreign Service Journal*  70
14th Amendment  22
Fox, Graham  112
Frank, Joanna  72
Funk, Laurence L. "Chucko"  58–59

Gagne, Paul  112
Gainey, Ryan  128, 134
Galloway cows  9, *76*, *116*–117
Galloway Ridge  10, 82, *84*, 87–*88*, 89, 117, 123
Gathering Place  9–10, 89–*90*, 93, 153
goats  10, 117–*118*
Godschalk, David  23
*Good Housekeeping*  8, 66–*67*
*Gourmet* magazine  40, 70, 109, 111
Governors Club  20, 81, 139, 142
granary  8, 36, 98–*99*, *100*, 143
Granville  10, 87, 150, 153
Greenslade, Forrest  *121*
Gregory, Ginny  2, 4, 32, 38–39, 45, 54, 110–111, 116, 127–*128*, 132, 134
Gust, James  83

*Harper's Magazine*  70
Havens, Anne Fitch  65
Heiser, Will  146
Helms, Jesse  36
Henderson, Ken  39
Henderson Place  10, 87
*Herald Tribune*  *110*
*Hideaway Report*  113
Historic District  5, 8, 49, 51–52, 55, 66, *78*, 82–83, 120, 123, 147
Hobhouse, Penelope  130
Hodges, Luther, Jr.  34–35
Holton, Robert  149
Houston, Texas  23
Howard, Karen  91
Howes, Bo  150–151
Hunt, Jim  35
Hunt, William Lanier  130
Huntoon, Maxwell  19
Hurricane Fran  9, 146–148

**186**

## Index

incorporation 143–144
Industrial Revolution 22

Jackson, Anthony 158
Jefferson, Thomas 21
Jenny's Park 77, *133*, 151; *see also* Camden Park
John, Elton 130, 125
Johnson, Lady Bird 100, 130
Johnson, Will 61

Kamphoefner, Henry 51
Kidd, Sue Monk 101
Kildaire Farms 25
Kirby, Winston 144
The Knolls 5, 80, 87
Krasnow, Rose 65, 151, 153
Kreller, Jaye 49–50
Krugman, Paul 21

Lee, Howard 4, 35, 138, 140
Leister, Jack 24
Lewis, Edna 109–111, *110*
Lindemann, Kirstine 69
liquor-by-the-drink (mixed drinks) 9, 73, 136–140
Los Angeles 22

mail kiosks 62, 91, 141, 153
Malacinski, George 69
Manjoo, Farhad 156
Marlow, Jane 65
Mattson, Corey 112
McDaniel, Gilda 39
McIntyre's Book Store 100–*101*, *102*, 156
Mears, Donna 39
Mediamax 70, 71, 74
Megginson, Keith 20, 41, 65, 156
Mencken, H.L. 3–4, 158
Messick, Paul 4, 19
Metzguer Karen 93–95
Millgcroft 87, 122–123, 150
mixed drinks 9, 73, 136–140
mixed-use 19, 23
modernist architecture 47–51
Montgomery neighborhood 5, 87
Moose, Ruth 147
Morgan, Laura 37–*38*, 42, 44, 65, 71, 75, 98–99, 148, *155*
Moriarty, Gene 144

National Center for Health Statistics 71
*National Geographic* **76**, 117
National Public Radio 36
Newsbreak 74
North Carolina Board of Elections 74
North Carolina Botanical Garden 36, 64, 130

North Carolina Department of Transportation 145
North Carolina Nature Conservancy 36
NC State University 16, 46, 51, 128–130, 156
N.C. Supreme Court 138
North Carolina Symphony 157
North Langdon Trail 122
Northwestern University 151
Norwood, Blake 145
Neal, Bill 8, 45, 107
Neal, Moreton 8, 43, 45, 106, 107
Nesbo, Jo 101
New York City 22
*New York Times* 21, 68, 72, 98, 142, 156
*New Yorker* 8, 68–75
*News & Observer* 12, 23, 86, 153, 155, 158
Nicolson, Harold 129
*North Carolina Architects & Builders* 51
Nyimicz, Daneen 63

Oakley, Hubert 26
Oglethorpe, James 52, 83
Oldham, John 15
Olmsted, Frederick Law 133
Orange County 19–20, 55, 63, 66, 71, 127

Paddleford, Clementine 110
Paycheck Protection Program 39
Penny, Grace 89
Perdue, Bev 35
Pew Research Center 72
Pitt, William (the elder) 7
Pitt, William (the younger) 7
Pittsboro 74, 142, 145, 148, 157
*Pittsboro Herald* 21–22, 25
Planned Unit Development (PUD) 8–9, 17, 19, 21–22, 24–26, 83, 87, 89, 91
Playmakers 157
Polk's Landing 57–59
Portman, Rob 35
Powell, Dannye Romine 101
Price, David 35
Price, Ed 65
Price, Marva 65, 147–148
Pringle, Jim 98

Quayle, Dan 100

Raleigh 3, 12, 16, 19, 23–24, 33, 37, 45, 47, 69, 73–74, 112, 115, 129, 145, 148, 155–157
Raleigh-Durham International Airport 11, 138–139
Raulston, J.C. 129–130
Redfin 74
Reed, Warren (Gus) 20
Rehm, Diane 101
Relais & Chateaux 111–*113*, 115

**187**

# Index

La Residence 8, 45, 107, 111
*Restaurants and Hotel Design* 47
Reston, Virginia 23, 96
Richmond neighborhood 5, 82,
Riddle, Jeanne 146, 148
Rigsbee, Randall 12
The Roost 4, 126, 156
Rosslyn Business Improvement District 24
Royal, Walter 111–112

Sackville-West, Vita 129
San Francisco 22
Sanyal, Deepa 69
Savannah, Georgia 52, 83, **85**
Schecter, Arielle 48–50
Schneider, Kim 94
Sears, Dan 4, 37, 39, 42–44, *43*, *46*, 50, 52–53, 79–83
Shearing, George 138
Shriver, Eunice Kennedy 149
Siler City 20, 31, 49, 139
Silverman, Emily 2
Simon, Robert E. Jr. 23
Simon Thomas, Maarten 122, 124
Sissinghurst 129
Smart, George 48
Smart Growth America 23
SmartAsset 74
Smith, Louis 16
solar houses 8, 59–60, 66
*Southern Living* 8, 47, 66, 80
special ABC areas 138–140
Special Olympics 10, 148–149
Steinem, Gloria 101
Stephens, Warren 112
Stromee, Carl 146
Stroud, Bob, "Farmer Bob" 10, 117
Sullivan, Barbara, 93
Summerson, Mandy 93
Surface, Michael 22
Sutton, Claire 58
Swim & Croquet 8–9, 90

*The Taste of Country Cooking* 109
Texas 23, 29, 154, 156
Thomas, Maarten Simon 122, ***124***
Thompson, Earl 26
Tippett, Rebecca 154–155
Toll, Robert 33
*Travel + Leisure Magazine* 115

*Triangle Business Journal* 115
Triangle J Council of Governments 24
Triangle Land Conservancy 150
Trump, Donald 36

U.S. Census Bureau 67, 71–72, 74–75, 154, 156
U.S. Postal Service 62, 141
U.S. Supreme Court 22–23
University of North Carolina 4, 11, 17, 19, 23, 27–28, 31, 37, 50, 55, 64, 73, 93, 103, 137, 151, 154, 156
University of Wisconsin Population Health Institute 71–72
*U.S. News & World Report* 115

Verey, Rosemary 129–130, 135
Village to Village 93
Village Way 11, 20, 79, 91, 96, 98, 123
Vinfast 157
Vinroot, Richard 35
Voices of Chatham 157

Wait, John 90
Wake County 20, 55, 66, 71, 73, 139
*Wall Street Journal* 68, 70
Wargin, Bill 64, 71
Wargin, Jill 64, 141, 142
*Washington Post* 71
wastewater treatment 8, 144–145
Weathersfield neighborhood 5, 9, 29, 79, 82, 89, 145, 153
Webster, John 126, 135
Wethersfield, England 29
Wilkins, Gloria 89
Williams, R.B. 83
Wimberley, Ben 26
*Wine Spectator* 137
Wolfspeed 157
The Woods neighborhood 9, 83
Wrenn, June 25–26
Wright, Frank Lloyd 48, 51
WUNC 36; *see also* National Public Radio

Yeager, Regina 36

Zabor, Doug 20, 36, 55, 58–59
zoning 22–24

188

www.ingramcontent.com/pod-product-compliance
Ingram Content Group UK Ltd.
Pitfield, Milton Keynes, MK11 3LW, UK
UKHW042010140426
5217IPUK00015B/1093